The Birth, Care, and Feeding of a Local Church

DONALD J. MacNAIR

A CANON PRESS BOOK

BAKER BOOK HOUSE • Grand Rapids, Michigan

Copyright © 1971 by
Donald J. MacNair

Paperback edition printed April 1976
by Baker Book House Company

ISBN: 0-8010-5996-8

First Printing, February 1976
Second Printing, March 1977

Printed in the United States of America

Contents

Preface

"The church has outlived its usefulness!" In recent years these devastating words have been harshly screamed by many radical social activists and have been blindly accepted by many confused Christians and by most idealistic young people.

I believe that the church is revealed in the Bible as the body of Christ, which means that the church always exists when there are believers. I believe that the message of the church is revealed in the Bible as the one message which everyone in every age needs, which means that the biblical church cannot outlive its usefulness. I believe that the bond of the church is revealed in the Bible as the spiritual unity of all believers and is revealed to be specifically demonstrated as the visible body, the local church.

However, many churches today are no longer concerned with the biblical basis, the biblical message, or the biblical organization of the church. With sorrow I confess that the accusation is valid concerning these churches—they have indeed outlived their usefulness.

Further, even many evangelical churches, which are firmly committed to the biblical basis of the church, have paid little if any regard to the biblical organization of the church and have done little or nothing to communicate the biblical message to this generation. It is with the greatest sorrow that I confess that the accusation is valid concerning these churches—they, too, have indeed outlived their usefulness.

PREFACE

Since my salvation (during my high school days) I have always been firmly committed to the Bible as the final authority of faith and practice. Thus I early became convinced that there is a biblical basis for the church. God later called me to preach the gospel. In doing so he brought me face to face with the inadequacy of so many churches today. He also motivated me to restudy the biblical basis for the necessity of the church, the biblical organization of the church, the relevance of the biblical message to our generation, and further, to determine ways and means of establishing churches in today's society (particularly in the United States of America) which will not depart from their God-given usefulness.

This book is the product of that study. It is also the product of years of applying the results of that research by actually establishing and nurturing congregations throughout the country. All the problems, heartaches, and successes of these experiences have in turn caused me constantly to refine the principles and to extend the breadth of the study itself. This is therefore a "how to do it" book.

But no use of methodology, no matter how expert, will ever produce a biblical church. Methodology is but a tool. The spiritual convictions upon which the methods rest for their strength must be comprehended and exercised if the use of these methods is to be valid. These convictions rest upon God's revelation of himself and of his promise:

> Remember the former things of old: for I am God, and there is none else; I am God, and there is none like me, Declaring the end from the beginning, and from ancient times the things that are not yet done, saying, My counsel shall stand, and *I will do all my pleasure.* (Isaiah 46:9-10)

In making this study and in putting the results into practice I have been guided by the Apostle Paul, who declared:

> Brethren, I count not myself to have apprehended: but this one thing I do, forgetting those things which are behind, and reaching forth unto those things which are before, *I press* toward the mark for the prize of the high calling of God in Christ Jesus. (Philippians 3:13-14)

To put it another way, the prerequisite convictions for those who would use this book are that they believe that God has a total plan and that his sovereign power will execute it; yet, nonetheless, he made us responsible for our own actions so that we must seek to know his will and earnestly, energetically carry out his will to the best of our ability. Throughout this book I have used Scripture verses in order to assure the reader that the propositions made are based on the Bible. I have also used Scripture verses to reinforce propositions and statements. However, this book is not designed to be a theological treatise on the doctrine of the church or on related doctrines to which I have occasionally made reference. The reader can find such a presentation in almost any standard theological textbook.

Even though this book is primarily designed for those involved in establishing new churches, I believe it will also be of value to churches which are already established and to their pastors. This is most apparent in the chapters dealing with the development of the church, the constitution and bylaws, the building structure, and the mother-daughter and church satellite programs for the extension of the church.

I would count it a privilege to hear from you who use this book about your experiences in establishing and extending churches and of the modifications or additions to the methods of this book which you have found useful.

I earnestly pray that God will use this book to bring glory to his name.

DONALD J. MACNAIR

Definitions

Seed families: families who band together to establish a church. All of them:

- are professing Christians;
- have an evident concern for the lost;
- are oriented at least to the theory of the system of doctrine and the form of government of the church to be established;
- and are convinced that they must take part in establishing such a church.

Mission church: a group of believers who, within several months to two years, seek to demonstrate both among themselves and through themselves to the world that God has indeed developed them into a self-sustaining particular church.

Particular church: a self-governing and self-sustaining body of believers who faithfully proclaim the whole counsel of God, properly administer the sacraments, and humbly submit themselves to discipline.

Elder: an ordained man, charged primarily with the responsibility of spiritual oversight of church members. Although churches often use different terms for this office, the term "elder" is used in this book.

Committee on assessment: a committee of two or three men, not of the seed families, who evaluate each phase in the development of the work, determine whether or not the group should go on to the next phase, and occasionally give counsel to the group. Throughout this book, this term is used for every contingency, thus including the executives of denominational church extension boards who may do this work professionally.

Community: the geographical area surrounding a church; and, a group of people who live within easy access of at least one common geographical point, all of whom have some aspect of their lives in common with each other. The geographical area surrounding a church will almost always include several such communities.

Rules of thumb: use of large gifts and grants; how adequately to pay the pastor; how to determine pastor's taxable income; formula for missions giving; formula for anticipating future size of congregation; axioms governing church life; pledges and mortgages in the building program; and formula for estimating cost of sanctuary.

Scripture quotations are from the King James Version, unless otherwise indicated.

Introduction

This book presents a plan by which believers can establish a church. It details this plan by defining basic concepts and developing them in consequential order. Further, in most cases is provides practical and proven methods to demonstrate how to apply these concepts.

The use of this material is most valuable when these concepts are considered in their proper sequence in the overall plan. To accomplish this it is necessary to present the overall plan at the outset. But even that isn't quite enough. It must be presented in such a way that it is easily grasped and just as easily remembered (even memorized).

Since the overall plan is in essence a timetable, it can be reduced to a chart (see accompanying figure: "The Overall Plan for Establishing a Church"). Experience in using this chart has demonstrated that it is easily comprehended and remembered.

Experience in using this chart has also demonstrated its value as both a goal and a "measuring stick" to the people actually involved in the ministry of establishing a new church. By constantly reviewing it they have been able to keep their priorities in order, and they have been able to determine whether or not they have been making significant progress.

Examine the chart carefully. It will be explained from left to right.

Before beginning that explanation, however, some comments on the use of the Functions of the Church are necessary. These functions are described in chapter one of the companion book: *The Growing Local Church*.[1]

THE OVERALL PLAN FOR ESTABLISHING A CHURCH

THE FOUR FUNCTIONS OF A CHURCH

WORSHIP
GROWTH IN GRACE
- Instruction
- Sanctification
- Fellowship

OUTREACH
- Evangelism
- Missions
- Community Involvement

ACTS OF MERCY
- Diaconate
- Community and World Concern

A		B		C	

PHASE I
Locate Seed Families and Establish the Mission Church

PHASE II
Organize

PHASE III
The Particular Church

LOCATE INITIAL FAMILIES

GET MORE PEOPLE

OBJECTIVE ASSESSMENT

DRAFT:
- Constitution
- Bylaws
- Statement of Specific Purpose

TRAIN MEN FOR OFFICERSHIP

OBJECTIVE ASSESSMENT

THE ESTABLISHED CHURCH CARRIES ON

A	B	C
Two Weeks On...		
One to Three Years	Nine to Twelve Months	Until the Lord Returns

FUNCTIONS OF THE CHURCH

Line "A-A" is the point at which the unorganized group of believers decide that they should attempt to establish a church. It is the beginning of the mission church.

As to when to start the Functions of the Church, the answer is that immediately upon making the decision to become a mission church they all must be operative. As to the intensity of the use of each one, common sense dictates that no church constantly practices them with equal intensity. But, they all must be simultaneously, as well as constantly, used.

Of most importance in the use of the functions is that the fruit of their use is the development of organism[2] in the church. It should be noted that as much as possible, organization[3] is put off until organism is evident. To supply government and organizational direction during this period, elders are borrowed (see chapter eleven).

CHART EXPLANATION

LOCATING THE INITIAL FAMILIES

Methods are described in chapters five, seven and, by inference, chapter fifteen. Note that no particular number of families must be committed to attempt to establish a church. Also note that these families may or may not be "seed families."[4] A minimum of seed families are needed to pass from phase one to phase two. That assessment is not normally made before the mission church is initially established. The development of organism in phase one is a major factor in helping families to become "seed families."

PHASE I—LOCATING SEED FAMILIES AND ESTABLISHING THE MISSION CHURCH

It will take almost all the time and *energy* of the mission church during phase one just to institute the Functions of the Church. All the remaining energy of the mission church must be used to reach more people! Chapters nine, ten, eleven, twelve, and fifteen deal with this experience.

---

1. Donald J. MacNair, *The Growing Local Church*. (Grand Rapids: Canon Press, Baker Book House, 1975).
2. MacNair, *Growing Local Church*, chap. 1.
3. MacNair, *Growing Local Church*, chap. 1.
4. Cf., chapter 4, page 21.

PHASE I—OBJECTIVE ASSESSMENT

See chapter five and chapter eight.

LINE "B-B"

This is the point in time that the Committee of Assessment[5] determines that the mission church should add to its work the task of preparing to be a self-governing church and to train men for officership in the church.

PHASE II—ORGANIZATION

See chapters thirteen, fourteen, and fifteen. (Note: a refinement has been made in the material on page twenty-one in this edition of *The Birth, Care, and Feeding of a Local Church*.)

PHASE II—OBJECTIVE ASSESSMENT

See chapters sixteen and seventeen.

LINE "C-C"

This is the point in time that the Committee on Assessment determines that the mission church should be constituted an established church and proceeds to do so. Chapters eighteen and nineteen will be of help to the new, particular church.

NOTE: There are no further vertical lines to this chart. The right side of the chart is unlimited. The local church should continue to exist as a part of the visible body of Christ until His return.

---

5. Cf., chapter 6.

1
Why Bother
With Churches Today?

This book is based on the premise that the church is mandatory, today as in any other day.

The word "church" is used in this book in the scriptural and historical sense to mean believers in Jesus Christ, gathered together in a visible, local group, who faithfully proclaim the whole counsel of God, properly administer the sacraments, and humbly submit themselves to discipline, to the end that God is glorified by the extension of his Kingdom and the rejoicing of his saints in their Lord.

In order to accept the premise that even today the church is mandatory, it is imperative properly to understand the Great Commission (Matthew 28:18-20). All too often it is thought to be merely a directive to foreign missions or to evangelism, so that if these ministries are carried out it is thought that the commission has been fulfilled. But the fact is that in the commission Christ has directed his disciples to do the very things the Bible declares to be the function of the church. Therefore, to fulfill the Great Commission demands the continual establishment of new churches: that is, the extension of the church.*

> All power is given unto me in heaven and in earth. Go now and make disciples of all nations, baptizing them in the name of the

---

* See chapter 2.

1

Father, and of the Son, and of the Holy Ghost: Teaching them to observe all things whatsoever I have commanded you: and, lo, I am with you alway even unto the end of the world. (Note: the beginning of verse 19 has been freely translated. Matthew 28: 18-20)

The commission is based on the infinite, eternal, and unchangeable power of Christ which is set forth in verse 18. Without this foundation verses 19 and 20 would be meaningless. Christ is not saying to this tiny handful of men: "You must increase your numbers quickly in order to develop a platform from which to command a hearing. Then you can wield the power of size, of organized lobbying, and of financial solutions for the problems of mankind in order to fulfill the purpose of the church." Rather, he is declaring that the power which the disciples need for success is *already present* and that consequently they will be able to fulfill his commission. Since this power is still present in Christ, today's disciples also may be assured that no ministry which is truly dependent on the power of Jesus Christ will fail.

The Lord now instructs his disciples that they are accountable to use the power of God. The disciples are given a commission which is applicable wherever they are. All of the disciples are given the same commission, since Christ does not direct only one or two "special" disciples to go to some particular place. Further, all the disciples are given a commission which requires them to do specific things.

The first specific requirement that Christ gives is that his disciples are to make disciples of (to "disciple") all nations. The task of making a disciple of Christ begins with evangelism to bring a person to Christ and into the relation of pupil to teacher. It goes on to include the development of the convert under the authority of God's Word so that he submits to the will of God. Making disciples, therefore, starts by evangelizing constantly and everywhere in order that God's own be won. But the rebirth of a soul is only the beginning. The convert is a baby: he must be loved, cared for, nurtured, disciplined and encouraged, until he can walk by himself in the Lord. How can he be a disciple, a follower, if he cannot yet walk? The Lord directs his disciples to undertake much more than evangelism in order to fulfill the commission. He directs them to disciple: to undertake all the work necessary to have the convert grow up to be a disciple himself, who in turn is commissioned to disciple still others.

The Lord then directs his followers to mark this convert by baptism: i.e., to brand him as now being in God and as separate from the world. When the meaning of baptism is understood, it becomes clear that this mandate indicates the need of the church. Baptism is not simply a social amenity. It is a sacrament given by God to his church. It requires a holy vow testifying that Jesus is Savior and submitting to him as Lord. And it assumes that there is a church, with its worship and discipline, which enables the disciple to carry out the implications of his vow.

The Lord continues his commission with the directive to teach the baptized convert to observe all the things he has commanded. The scope of this teaching includes:

- what the Christian is to believe about God: who God is, how he works, how he revealed himself, how he reconciles men to himself, etc.

- how the Christian is to live: being fulfilled by the love of God, demonstrating the love of God to his fellow Christians and to those who are not Christians, obeying his will, overcoming temptation, defending the faith steadfastly, anticipating the Lord's return, etc.

The scope of this teaching is so great that the task of teaching will continue, in one way or another, throughout his life. (It could never be accomplished in one or two teaching sessions, as would be possible if evangelism alone fulfilled the commission!)

This command to "observe" also brings the concept of discipline into play again. The church must do more than make pronouncements about righteousness; it dare never try to achieve righteousness by legislation. It must teach with love and support its teaching with discipline.

The Lord concludes the commission with the promise that he is always with the Christian, thus providing him the power necessary to fulfill the commission in every age. In the commission Christ has given his disciples those specific directives which are the task of the church: to make disciples, to baptize and to teach. In these directives are comprehended the presentation of the whole counsel of God, the proper dispensation of the sacraments and the necessity to practice discipline. Hence the conclusion that the church is mandatory even today. In order to fulfill the commission wherever the Christian goes, therefore, he must establish new churches in each place. This is the imperative which has been given to every Christian; therefore, it has been given to today's Christians.

2
The Universal Purpose
of the Church

There is only one universal purpose of Christ's church throughout the world. This book primarily deals not with the universal purpose, but with the particular purpose of a local, visible church. The particular purpose is actually a specific application of the universal purpose to a local situation. In no way does it replace, even in part, the universal purpose. Rather, it must be the means by which the universal purpose is achieved locally. In order fully to appreciate this relationship, the universal purpose of the church must be defined and explained.

The universal purpose of the church is based on the Bible's concept of the church itself. The definition of the church that will be used is derived from the relationship of God's people to himself during their earthly pilgrimage.

A church is a body of believers brought together by the Holy Spirit as a visible part of the body of Christ, who faithfully proclaim the whole counsel of God, properly administer the sacraments and humbly submit themselves to discipline, all for the glory of God.

From this definition the universal purpose of the church becomes evident. In broadest terms, it is to glorify God. More precisely, it is

---

* Scripture references in this chapter are from the New American Standard Bible.

5

to reconcile God and man, with all the biblical consequences that naturally result from that reconciliation.

This chapter will first discuss the universal purpose in the broad sense of glorifying God, and then in the more specific sense of reconciling God and man. Finally, the universal purpose in terms of its practical application will be discussed.

The broadest expression of the universal purpose of the church is that the church exists for the glory of God. "Worthy art Thou, our Lord and our God, to receive glory and honor and power; for Thou didst create all things, and because of Thy will they existed, and were created" (Revelation 4:11). Now to the King eternal, immortal, invisible, the only God, be honor and glory forever and ever. Amen" (1 Timothy 1:17).

This task of giving honor and glory to God is basic to everything in life and therefore basic to the church. "... He chose us in Him before the foundation of the world, that we should be holy and blameless before Him. In love He predestined us to adoption as sons through Jesus Christ to Himself, according to the kind intention of His will, to the praise of the glory of His grace, which He freely bestowed on us in the Beloved" (Ephesians 1:4-6). God "made us alive together with Christ ... in order that in the ages to come He might show the surpassing riches of His grace in kindness toward us in Christ Jesus" (Ephesians 2:7). From these verses it is clear that the church does indeed exist for the glory of God.

Next, this broad statement of purpose may be more precisely stated in the light of the relationship God the Father has provided sinful man through God the Son, Jesus Christ. In Jesus, God and man are reconciled.

"Therefore if any man is in Christ, he is a new creature; the old things passed away; behold, new things have come. Now all these things are from God, who reconciled us to Himself through Christ, and gave us the ministry of reconciliation, namely, that God was in Christ reconciling the world to Himself, not counting their trespasses against them, and He has committed to us the word of reconciliation" (2 Corinthians 5:17-19).

"For it was the Father's good pleasure for all the fullness to dwell in Him, and through Him to reconcile all things to Himself, having made peace through the blood of His cross; through Him, I say, whether things on earth or things in heaven" (Colossians 1:19-20).

Reconciliation therefore makes man a new creature. As such he can relate to God as his father for the first time, and thus is able to worship God.* And it is his local church which provides the communion of the saints that is necessary for his corporate worship.

As a new creature the Christian now can freely respond to the will of God for the first time. His entire life is now redirected. Through his reconciliation to God he can now freely respond to God's love by being reconciled to other men and by participating in bringing all of creation to the point of finding its true head in Christ. Again, his local church provides the community of the saints which is necessary at least to initiate, orient and foster this response.

Finally, as a new creature now freely able to respond to the will of God, he will become directly involved in reaching the lost with the gospel.

If the universal purpose of the church is in broad terms to glorify God, it is more precisely expressed as the reconciliation of God and man. This reconciliation must be clearly understood if the relationship between the universal purpose and the particular purpose of the church is to be understood. Therefore we should now examine this concept more fully.

Hebrews 10:25 clearly declares that Christians must meet together in a corporate relationship ("not forsaking our own assembling together, as is the habit of some, but encouraging one another; and all the more, as you see the day drawing near"). Among many implications, this admonition recognizes the necessity for Christians to share in those blessings which are peculiar to the corporate worship of the visible church. For instance, only in corporate worship does the full reality of communion among the saints as well as communion of each Christian with his Lord become our experience. The Lord has promised not only to indwell each individual Christian, but also to be in the midst of a group of believers (Matthew 18:20).

---

* See chapter 5 for a discussion of worship.

Possibly the greatest blessing resulting from corporate worship is the fact that the Lord uses it to establish a foundation upon which the Holy Spirit employs individual Christians in his building and his sanctifying ministry. It is precisely at this point that our reconciliation with God really extends to cause our reconciliation with men.

As men worship our Lord together the Spirit both breaks down walls of partition between them and inspires them to new attitudes toward each other: they will value each other more as made in God's image, they will be more sensitive to each others' needs, and their love for each other will be more Christlike. "By this all men will know that you are My disciples, if you have love for one another" (John 13:35).

In this context the Holy Spirit uses the gifts and talents of individual Christians to build up each other in his grace. "But to each one is given the manifestation of the Spirit for the common good" (1 Corinthians 12:7). "Love ... does not seek its own ... rejoices with the truth; bears all things, believes all things, hopes all things, endures all things" (1 Corinthians 13:4-7). This develops the community* of the church which is unique from anything else on the face of the earth.

A word of warning is needed before going on. All too often, a misconception of this true communion of the saints is permitted to develop. Most frequently it is called "fellowship." Although this word in itself is a good synonym for communion, it will be used here to describe the misconception which fails to recognize that true communion involves the Holy Spirit's ministry in and through believers unto their sanctification. The ultimate tragedy occurs when the value of this "fellowship" (in the misused sense) is permitted not only to abort true communion, but when it is raised to be of equal or even greater importance than worship itself.

Because reconciliation makes participating in the work of santification possible, this misunderstanding must be recognized and checked. Christianity means a new birth, a radical change by the grace of God. A

---

* The term "community" is used in several ways in this book. In addition to the interpersonal experience described here, it is primarily used (cf. chapter 5) for the concept of community of interest in a given geographical area (See Definitions and Rules of Thumb). Care must be taken to differentiate.

local church, through its mere existence, provides the basis for Christians to be with each other, and, on the basis of their shared relationship to Christ, to form deep and meaningful friendships. But all too often these friendships become the only fulfilling consequence of church membership and corporate worship. When this occurs, the universal purpose of that local church soon becomes "fellowship" in the distorted sense.

This unbiblical and unfortunate misunderstanding of the purpose of the church usually develops because of the influence of two weaknesses in contemporary Christian life.

1. Many Christians have failed to learn, through lack of Bible study or the superficial use of the Bible and of prayer, how to appropriate the daily grace of God. For instance, young people today are influenced from every point of authority and counsel to live amorally. The Bible teaches that God's grace to withstand such pressure is appropriated as follows: "Put on the full armor of God, that you may be able to stand firm against the schemes of the devil: ... truth, ... righteousness, ... the gospel of peace, ... faith, ... salvation, ... and the sword of the Spirit, which is the word of God" (Ephesians 6:11, 13-17). However, in churches where "fellowship" is misunderstood, children of believers come to believe that their spiritual armor is found by depending upon their Christian peers.

2. Christians today are more and more dissatisfied with lives that do not fulfill their spiritual as well as physical needs. But many have failed to learn that they can find true fulfillment only in the experience of a constantly deepening walk with Christ through all the areas of life. The Bible teaches that this is accomplished only when everything that we are is given to God as a living experience of sacrifice. "I urge you therefore, brethren, by the mercies of God, to present your bodies a living and holy sacrifice, acceptable to God, which is your spiritual service of worship. And do not be conformed to this world, but be transformed by the renewing of your mind, that you may prove what the will of God is, that which is good and acceptable and perfect" (Romans 12:1-2). This involves being transformed by the renewing of our minds. Observe the contrast in meanings of "fellowship" above.

In many churches the programs and activities, especially those having spiritual goals, provide the only spiritual fulfillment that many church members find. Then, because the members are spending much time together, sharing the work and activity, a camaraderie—a "fellowship"— develops. They have unwittingly accepted a substitute for the experience of a constantly deepening walk with Christ. The end result is, of course, that this misunderstood "fellowship" has obscured the purpose of the church.

The communion of the saints, true fellowship, indeed is a tremendous blessing provided through the goodness of the Lord. It is the result of individual and corporate worship. However, it is not, nor should we allow it to become, the sole purpose of the church.

Returning to the special blessing of the Spirit in the midst of believers, an additional consequence of our reconciliation to God is the participation of the body of Christ in bringing all of creation to the point of finding its true head in Christ. It is precisely at this point that our reconciliation to God causes us to appreciate God's work in reconciling all of his creation to himself.

Upon Christ's return this will be fully accomplished. "For the creation was subjected to futility, not of its own will, but because of him who subjected it, in hope that the creation itself also will be set free from its slavery to corruption into the freedom of the glory of the children of God. For we know that the whole creation groans and suffers the pains of childbirth together until now" (Romans 8:20-21). Until then, the curse is still devastating the world. Yet, through the church, the creatures of heaven and men in the world see a witness that will hold them accountable to acknowledge the headship of Christ. Also, through the ministry of the church, the total scope of man's creativity is demonstrated in a new light. Art, architecture, science, engineering, etc., all must be tools of the Christian and the church, and man's achievements must be applied by the Christian and the church.

A direct involvement of the church in serving its Lord as reconciled men is the task of reaching the lost with the gospel. In this regard, the church has been both changed by and challenged with the Great Commission.* Its ultimate fulfillment begins with evangelism and goes

---

* See chapter 1.

on to include the follow-up in disciple training, the proper use of the sacraments, and the continued teaching of all that Christ has taught (which of course includes the exercise of discipline). Its ultimate fulfillment therefore demands the establishment and extension of the church. This is the biblical concept of presenting the gospel to the lost. This is real outreach—nothing less is sufficient!

Reconciliation of God and man has been shown to be the specific expression of the universal purpose of the church. This presentation of universal purpose would be incomplete, however, if it were not pointed out that the Bible declares the specific content of the message of reconciliation. It can be summed up by two phrases: the Bible reveals what man is to believe concerning God and what God requires of man. Putting it another way, the Bible reveals the doctrinal and governmental truths necessary for individual salvation and for individual and corporate life after salvation. These truths are often referred to as the standards of a church. When using these standards in the course of God's work of reconciliation the universal purpose of the church becomes practical. This use of the standards actually provides two guides for achieving the universal purpose of the church at the congregational level.

First, the very presence of the standards gives the church positive direction. They express in logical order and in some detail the practical implications of the doctrine of reconciliation. Thus they enable the church to relate its faith and practice to the challenges it faces every day.

Second, the very presence of the standards gives the church positive boundaries beyond which it may not go in expressing its faith or exercising its government. Standards outline clearly the system of doctrine and the form of government of the church. If the church is truly committed to its standards, they act as boundaries to restrain it from going into apostasy.

It must be pointed out, however, that it is also precisely at the point of using standards that the universal purpose of the church has often become obscured, distorted and even crushed out of existence. Two major forces bring this about:

    1. One of these forces stems from the differences between the

standards of various churches. As to the doctrinal standards, for example, some are Calvinistic and others are Arminian. As to governmental standards, some are hierarchical, some democratic and others republican. The very fact that there are differences of opinion encourages churches to spend an inordinate amount of time defending their own position, thus easily obscuring the magnitude of God's work of reconciliation. It is true that these differences are real and cannot be ignored. However, no church should concern itself so much with defending its distinctives that this defense appears to be its purpose for existence.

Also, the fact that there are differences of opinion tends to make it easy for some Christians to adopt an exclusive attitude toward other Christians, which in turn obscures the magnitude of God's work of reconciliation. The standards to which church officers swear allegiance by means of their ordination vows are indeed important, but every Christian must remember that salvation rests upon childlike faith in Jesus as one's Savior and Lord, not on the precision with which we can articulate our particular system of doctrine and form of government.

2. The other of these forces stems from the lack of commitment to biblical standards. When standards are not maintained, heretical and even apostate positions almost always arise. Many contemporary churchmen are rejecting the very work of reconciliation, the church's universal purpose itself. These men reject the Bible as the inspired, infallible Word of God. Consequently they have no objection to redefining the purpose of the church. They almost universally declare that biblical reconciliation is concerned with reconciling man to man without reference to reconciling God and man.

A sad spin-off of this force is that this heresy has been so effectively promulgated that many true believers, weary of fighting it, are accepting watered-down doctrinal and governmental standards simply in order to have any standards at all. These standards then become the expression of their emasculated understanding of the purpose of their church. Therefore, this satanic force is succeeding in at least obscuring the universal purpose in many places where it has not succeeded in crushing it.

The universal purpose of the church is clear: to bring glory to God; to reconcile God and man, with all the biblical consequences that naturally result from that reconciliation. In order to accomplish this universal purpose most efficiently in its own situation, the local church determines its own particular purpose.

3
The Particular Church
Must Have a Particular Purpose

The phrase "particular church" will be used for a body of believers, worshiping together, who are in fact a truly biblical church. To be specific, a particular church is a body of believers brought together by the Holy Spirit as a visible part of the body of Christ, who faithfully proclaim the whole counsel of God, properly administer the sacraments and humbly submit themselves to discipline, all for the glory of God.

Men are involved, not in starting a church, but in establishing it. God has started it by preparing the manpower and the motivation long before anyone is aware of the possibility of a new church. Therefore this book is designed to present the program for men to follow in establishing churches.

The particular church is distinguished by at least two major features. (It should be noted that these distinguishing features do not depend on the extent of the talents and achievements of the congregation and/or the pastor!) One is that the people and the pastor are committed to the convictions that:

- they are indeed part of the body of Christ;

- the Bible is the written Word of God, verbally inspired in the original, and the only rule of faith and practice;

- the task of the church is to be used of God to reconcile men to himself, by actively engaging in reaching the lost for Christ and building up the Christian in Christ.

- the gospel must be proclaimed to the lost in any way necessary to communicate successfully to our contemporaries;

- the lives of the pastor and people must demonstrate the fruits of the Spirit, with very evident expressions of love and tenderness;

- provision for safeguarding the development of the church has been made in the office of the elder, to whom the Bible assigns the responsibility for doctrine and government. The authority has been conferred upon him through the oath of ordination.

The convictions motivate the church, both as individual members and as a corporate whole, to a practice of life which admits to the Lordship of Christ.

The other distinguishing feature of the particular church is that the individual members, being constantly "fitted together" by the work of the Holy Spirit, are daily "growing into a holy temple of the Lord" (Ephesians 2:20, ASV). That is to say, the outside world looking on will recognize that God is living in and among the members of the church because of the unity of mind and heart the members demonstrate. Further, it is to say that it has become evident to the members themselves that God is living in and among them so that the church has become their spiritual home where they are finding an expression of precious love one to the other, a center of genuine concern for each other, a sanctuary of community worship which is neither shallow nor restrained, and a haven for the unsaved.

Although all particular churches share these two essential features, still there is wide latitude for diversity in the impression made by the church on the non-member. There are five factors which influence the outsiders' opinion of the particular church: the worship, the people, the programs, the building(s), and the ultimate size. Whether the observer sees only one of these factors or studies carefully all five of them, it is on the basis of his impressions in these areas that he draws his conclusions as to what kinds of people make up the church and what concern they have for their God and for the non-member.

Each particular church automatically projects an impression of some kind. In order to capitalize on this fact, each particular church should seek to develop itself so as to convey that particular impression which it believes most successfully demonstrates why it exists and how it intends to accomplish the purpose for its existence.

This effort, in turn, makes it necessary to draft a statement which sets forth the specific purpose agreed upon by the church. This declaration expresses how a local body of God's people believes their church should conduct itself so that it is both a truly biblical church and the most relevant possible church for their specific community.

This declaration must first be drafted in the earliest stages of the church's development even though it will probably be refined, enlarged or even changed many times in the future.

The declaration of specific purpose is based on a consensus of opinion that demonstrates what expression of the five factors of influence:

* most fulfills the members;
* most adequately demonstrates what concern the church member has for his God and for the non-member;
* and most successfully serves as a meaningful communication to the community which the church anticipates reaching.

The declaration of specific purpose adopted by the particular church is only meaningful when it is based on the commitment to those approaches to church life and outreach which will best achieve the purpose.

In drafting the statement every church must take into account these basic principles as fundamental:

* The reality and the character of God must be emphasized.
* The reality of living by faith also must be emphasized.
* The use of boldness and imagination must always be kept within the boundaries defined by the church's system of doctrine and government. (It must be noted that, without these boundaries, the exercise of boldness and imagination will eventually bring about a departure from the biblical basis for the church, rather than an enrichment of the impression given by this particular church. On the other hand, any practice, even if it has never been tried before by anyone else anywhere, which reflects the reality of God and

the faith of the church, and which does not conflict with the system of doctrine nor the government of the church, would be acceptable in accomplishing the church's specific purpose.)

The declaration of specific purpose will reflect such major concepts as whether the church is to be oriented to a rural, a suburban, an urban, or an inner city ministry; whether the church wants to remain relatively small in the future; whether the order and conduct of the worship services will receive special attention; etc.

This declaration of specific purpose will serve as a guideline to assist the particular church in structuring its life and outreach. A danger must be pointed out with regard to any declaration of specific purpose, however: it is not a legalistic control or an unbreakable strait jacket. Putting it another way, it cannot be allowed to be a substitute for continued dependence on the Holy Spirit in the life and outreach of the church.

The significance of the declaration of specific purpose may be clarified by comparing a particular church to a person. The skeleton—solid bone—is the doctrine and government of the church; the breath of life is the evidence of the reality of God and of personal faith in him through Jesus Christ. However, what the world sees is the shape of the body. As the contour of the flesh around the skeleton is the outward manifestation of the person, obviously differing according to the individual, so the impression given by each church, though based on the skeletal doctrine, varies according to the specific purpose it has chosen.

As a guideline to assist the particular church in structuring its life and outreach, however, the declaration of specific purpose also provides a very vital tool for periodic evaluation of the work, which is so necessary. This evaluation will seek to determine whether the specific purpose agreed upon by the church is in fact being communicated, and with what degree of success it is being communicated. A difficulty must be pointed out: namely, that any program of evaluation is most unusual in church life and demands spiritual commitment to the basic principles among the seed families, if it is to be effective. For instance, the church must be spiritually mature enough to discontinue one activity (even though many have become accustomed to it and like it) and/or start a new activity, when it determines that such action is needed to enrich the church life and outreach. Again, the church must be spiritually mature enough to admit that world, nation, and community changes may force the church to consider reworking the very declaration of specific purpose itself in order that the church will continue to be related to life as it is currently lived.

IS ALL THIS REALLY NECESSARY?

The conditions of the world today are such that a church is in grave danger if it has not worked out a statement of its own position. The particular church must be clearly aware of its own particular purpose if it is to face the non-Christian community, if it is to stand firm in this age of ecumenism, and if it is to find its place in the evangelical world.

As each church faces its own community, it must demonstrate that it knows why it exists and how it intends to accomplish the purpose for its existence, if it is to be respected as a true church. The church that gives any other impression in the community will be viewed, by the very ones who need the gospel, either as just one more social organization or else merely as a "sect."

There are sincere Christians, unaware of the impression received by the unsaved, who fear that by deliberately determining a specific purpose for the church the work of the Holy Spirit is abrogated. They often express it thus: "The church exists simply to preach the gospel; to state a more specific purpose is extra-biblical."* This is not a realistic view, for it ignores the fact that the community will inevitably receive *some* impression of the church, whether it is given deliberately or not, and it will draw its own conclusions from this impression as to the purpose of the church. Only if the church has spelled out its own specific purpose clearly and only if it seeks to achieve this purpose in all aspects of church life, will it be able to give an impression which glorifies God in the eyes of the community.

Furthermore, such a view implies that the admonition to do all things "decently and in order" does not apply to this area of church development; it ignores the fact that the apostles gave admonitions in areas far beyond merely the preaching of the gospel and thereby taught

---

* This is a direct quotation of a statement made during a symposium in Wisconsin in 1970.

the church how to accomplish the purpose for which it exists. For example, when the Gentile Christians of the first century were in distress because of attempts of Judaizers to force them to be circumcised and to keep the Jewish law, the apostles and elders sent delegates to them with a letter instructing them how to conduct themselves in a manner consistent with their faith and with their particular situation:

> For it seemed good to the Holy Ghost, and to us, to lay upon you no greater burden than these necessary things; That ye abstain from meats offered to idols, and from blood, and from things strangled, and from fornication: from which if ye keep yourselves, ye shall do well. Fare ye well (Acts 15:28-29).

Second, today's spirit of ecumenism makes a declaration of specific purpose necessary. Each church must have a declaration of specific purpose if it is to maintain identity against the pressures to join the "one-church" movement which has substituted size and influence for biblical faith.

Finally, each church must hammer out its declaration of specific purpose if its members are to become fitted together in spite of the tensions in today's evangelical world. For example, in almost every mission church two differing approaches to worship are represented. One is characterized by the desire for worship with the benefit of the security that comes from familiar surroundings and experiences. Those with this point of view find it difficult to accept innovations in the order of worship with which they are familiar, or to accept anything other than a colonial church building, etc. The other approach is characterized by the desire for worship with the benefit of the challenge that comes from individually-structured forms of worship. Those with this point of view find it difficult to accept the routine order of worship week after week, the lack of participation by many of the members in conducting the worship, etc. However, these differing approaches to worship are not mutually exclusive. The people must come to appreciate the valuable influence which each attitude should exert on the other. Yet without a declaration of specific purpose the mission church will either adopt by default the attitude of the most persuasive group in the church, with the consequent loss of the other group, or else internal tensions will develop that will destroy all evidence of unity and solidarity.

4
Introducing
the Procedure

There are two basic ingredients needed in order to establish a church successfully. These basics cannot be avoided or even watered down. They are:

1. Eight to twelve "seed" families: Christian families already with *vision*, who:

   • are professing Christians;
   • have an evident concern for the lost;
   • are oriented at least to the theory of the system of doctrine and form of government of the church to be established;
   • and are convinced that they must take part in establishing such a church.

2. An organizing pastor: a teaching elder with *vision*, who is:

   • a qualified teaching elder;
   • concerned for the lost;
   • concerned for the growth of the Christian;
   • concerned for the blessings that come only from the interaction of families under the influence of the Holy Spirit working in the visible church;

- willing to work with abounding energy and imagination;
- a living communication of his vision;
- and a man of decision and action.

The procedure for establishing a church, using these two basic ingredients, is a program with these three phases:

I. LOCATING THE "SEED" FAMILIES AND ESTABLISHING THE MISSION CHURCH.

Taking as long as is necessary, a minimum of eight to twelve families are contacted and then oriented. They become convinced that they should be the "seed" families for a new church. The primary emphasis during this phase is to reach people, among whom will be the "seed" families.

When the decision is actually made to attempt to establish a church, a mission church is established. The families involved at that time are declaring that they anticipate becoming a particular church within a few months to no longer than four years, during which time they look to the Lord to multiply in number, grow in faith and in the Christian life, develop a progressively increasing outreach, properly train the manpower eventually to become the church officers, accept the responsibility for the purity and doctrinal position of the church, and then become self-governing, self-sustaining, and (de facto) a particular church.

II. ORGANIZATION.

The primary emphasis during this phase is to develop the organization necessary to maintain the organism already present. This would include drafting a constitution, bylaws, and a statement of specific purpose. It would also include training men for the office of elder and deacon.

III. ESTABLISHING THE PARTICULAR CHURCH.

The proper church authority, concurring with the conviction of the mission church itself, based on tangible evidence from the experience as a mission church, constitutes the mission church as a particular church.

5

Preparation to Use the Procedure

Even though the temptation almost always exists to capitalize *right now* on the zeal of interested people or special circumstances, a full comprehension of some of the "facts of life" involved, coupled with an in-depth survey of the actual field itself must precede any action on the scene.

Some of the "facts of life" include:

- At least eight to twelve seed families are needed (see chapter three for definition) in order to proceed with a mission church. One out of six families in the United States moves each year; God often brings one of the members of these families to himself during the course of a year; and several families could find the cost (financial, emotional and/or spiritual) of helping to establish a church too high during the first year. The net result is that often 25 to 50 percent of the original seed families will not be with the group after the first year. If the initial number of seed families is lower than eight, the number at any given time during the first year could be so low that the work would die by default if not by embarrassed disillusionment.

- The exact minimum number of families depends on varying circumstances. If the potential for growth seems very immediate, as few as eight families might be sufficient. If the cash flow of the group appears to be limited, at least ten or twelve families would be needed.

- By "family" the entire family unit is meant. This could mean a wage-earning single person of either sex or a family unit without the wife being active, but not a family in which the husband is not active.

- A budget between $1,000 to $1,200 per month will be needed to be realistic in financial matters. It would be used to:
  a. employ the organizing pastor;
  b. provide housing for the organizing pastor;
  c. have a missions fund of 2 to 4 percent of the undesignated general fund giving;
  d. rent a school or hall for Sunday worship, and pay for professional caretaker;
  e. supply basic materials (Sunday school literature, bulletins, etc.);
  f. advertise.

- The friends and relatives of the seed families are the people to whom the witness of Christ and this mission church must first be made. Any sense of fear to capitalize on this particular area of contact not only dooms the immediate growth potential of the mission church, but also undermines one of the cardinal motivating factors for establishing the church in the first place, namely, a concern for the lost. No church can succeed if in reality it is simply a "comfortable" place to be.

- Any new church will probably attract the church mavericks and church malcontents once it is started. The need to have new faces and additional income is often so great that the initial group becomes blinded to the fact that these people may become sources of trouble. No church will succeed, regardless of its numbers, income, or growth patterns, in bringing glory to God if it builds on people who simply "can't get along" or are always fighting and never engaged positively in the work of reaching the lost and edifying the saints. The church must be prepared for such people to visit and possibly become active. The church must of course offer spiritual help to them, but in doing so it must be sure to challenge them to be motivated by the positive position of the church before becoming active or else to recognize that they do not belong.

- God uses people with distinctive characteristics to do work in one place and others with differing distinctives in other places (e.g., people with a desire for a highly emotional form of worship as contrasted with those who desire formal, liturgical worship). It must be remembered that one group cannot do everything nor be everywhere, nor are those of differing expressions lesser groups in God's sight.
- All churches can be described as belonging to one of four categories: the inner city, the urban, the suburban and the rural churches. However, even within any one category, it does not stand to reason that simply because a given program was successful in one place it automatically will be successful in other places.

Next, an in-depth survey of the proposed field must be taken before any intelligent assessment of the possible development can be made. All too often this work is considered a non-spiritual, "worldly"-motivated approach to establishing a church and is either not done at all or is so poorly done that it produces data that really are only the prejudiced opinions of those involved.

The in-depth survey will give a knowledge of a proposed field that will not only guide in the initial decision whether or not to begin, but will assist in knowing where to place the greatest emphasis, how it should be done, when it should be done, where to locate, salary needed by an organizing pastor in order to live in the area, etc.

The in-depth survey gathers data upon which decisions can be made: as to the general type and strength of the area, and as to the spiritual and religious climate of the area. Suggested sources for the information are listed after each item.

A. General background data to be gathered.
1. Historical background of the area. A sketchy report is sufficient. (chamber of commerce)
2. Principal industries and businesses and any other principal sources of income of the area. (chamber of commerce)
3. Population growth-charts for the past ten years. (chamber of commerce)
4. Industrial and business growth charts for the past ten years

(chamber of commerce). Get comments on the economic stability of the area.

5. Prognostications for population growth and where it will be concentrated for the next two years, five years, ten years. (chamber of commerce, regional directors of utility companies, superintendent of schools, city and county planning commission. Note: Go to all of them in order to: a) compare results, b) get differing views, c) make personal contacts.)

6. Prognostications for industrial and business growth for the next two years, five years, ten years. (chamber of commerce, utility companies, city or county planning commission, heads of industries and businesses. Again, go to all of these.)

7. Survey of present population concentrations: as to location and major ethnic, religious and/or vocational characteristics. (chamber of commerce)

8. Survey of downtown: Is it an inner city? Does it have commercial desirability? Are rehabilitation programs being carried out, or at least prepared for? (chamber of commerce, city or county planning commission)

9. Degree of accessibility from all parts of the area, especially as to interstate and/or circumferential arteries.

10. Relative cost of living in the area. (real estate agent, chamber of commerce)

11. Cost of land and housing. (real estate agent)

12. Community attitude toward progress—e.g., passage of school tax issues for school buildings, teachers' salaries; planned zoning programs; tax incentive programs; etc. (superintendent of schools, chamber of commerce)

13. Permanence of residents in the community. What percentage remains only six months to two years? What percentage of new buildings are apartment houses as compared to individual homes? (chamber of commerce, city or county planning commission, real estate agent)

14. Cultural atmosphere of the area. Are there any colleges? universities? art and music programs? (chamber of commerce, the college dean)

The assessment to be made from these data must include consideration of the following questions:

   a. Is the overall community progressive, stagnant or decaying?

   b. Are there built-in barriers in the area that would have to be overcome before a new church could get a good start? (e.g., An area predominantly Jewish would demand an extended financial underwriting for the potential church to survive long enough to become self-sustaining. It is not realistic spiritually simply to point to the mass of people without Christ and say, "we" must succeed in establishing a church. Too many such attempts have died, leaving a bad testimony, before reaching enough of the lost all around them to grow strong enough to be self-sustaining.)

   c. Are there built-in potentials that would enable a new church quickly to become a known and respected identity in the community? (For instance, can the neighborhood use the church building as a polling place? Can the board of education of the public schools use the pastor or some of the church members on a citizens' committee to advise the board? etc.)

   d. In addition to these generalities, specific data about costs, land, culture, etc., must lead to a proposal as to the probable operating cost of a mission church for its first few months and a further proposal as to the minimum number of seed families needed to assure that the establishment of a mission church is indeed a step of faith and not presumption.

B. Religious data to be gathered.

   1. What is the history of churches of your persuasion in the area? Are there any doctrinally sound churches similar to yours already in the area? Was there any doctrinally sound witness of this kind within the past five years, ten years, fifteen years?

   2. If there are any churches of your persuasion in the area, where are they located and what is their specific program for evangelism? (Visit with pastor and session.)

   3. Are there any evangelical testimonies in the area? If so, where

are they and what are their outstanding characteristics? (Visit with some of the pastors.)

4. Are there any concentrations of one or more major denominations?

5. Is there a local council of churches? If so, how powerful is it?

6. Have a personal interview with all known contacts in the area. Make an appraisal as to their ability to serve as seed families if a mission church is to be started.

7. Seek the names of all new contacts (by referral from the known contacts and from anyone else interviewed during the survey). Have personal interviews and report as to their potentiality as seed families. (See Appendix E.)

8. Make a preliminary proposal of the best location for a church.

9. Determine the availability of rental space (schools, etc.) and cost per month, especially in relation to the preliminary suggestion of church site.

10. Make a suggestion based on the assessment of the survey data gathered as to the distinctive characteristics a church in this area should develop in order to be most effective in its witness.

The assessment to be made from the religious data gathered must include consideration of the following questions:

a. Are there already sufficient seed families to establish a mission church?

b. Can the seed families be used to structure the specific type of church program most needed for that community at this time?

c. Will all the effort involved really only produce one more church just like those already in the area, except that it would have a different name? If that is apparently the only potential, is such work

1) consistent with the distinctive purpose, and

2) is it really needed, or would it be simply a personal comfort to a few people?

Seed families come from five sources:

a. An existing church (and probably the pastor too) want to leave an existing denomination and become a particular church (either independent or denominational) *en masse.*

b. An existing church grows to the size that it would prefer to multiply itself by establishing a new church using some of its members, officers and money, rather than just grow larger and larger. (See chapter nineteen.)

c. Individuals and/or families, who are aware of the distinctive witness of your church and are seeking to be used as seed families ask for help to establish a mission church. (These families have either just moved to a new area and cannot find a church home to fit their needs, or they are unwilling to remain in their present church home because of liberalism, etc.)

d. A full-time missionary moves into an area and mounts a program of Bible classes, personal evangelism, children's work, etc., in an attempt to be used to reach people for Christ, to see them grow in grace and training, to locate Christian families living in the area who would be interested, and attempt within two or three years to have sufficient seed families with which to establish a mission church. This program is not to be confused with the way in which many denominations process their church extension: by giving a minister an area in which to labor, putting up a church building, providing an initial capital of $50,000 and expecting one hundred families within three years. This kind of church extension violates the biblical position that the church is the people, and therefore, until the people are present, involved and convinced that the hand of God is indeed on them, a true church does not yet even exist, much less call for a building.

e. An existing church or denomination, after an in-depth survey reveals that the potential is ripe for establishing a mission church, mounts a concentrated program, with much help, to accomplish in a short time what a lone missionary would normally take two to three years to accomplish. Much is done by a public presentation as well as visiting and Bible classes in this program. This program will utilize the massive canvass development program and/or the concentrated visitation-Bible class development program. (See chapter seven.)

From any of these sources, but especially from (a) or (c), families may appear who are apparently qualified to be seed families, but are primarily motivated only by a negative conviction. Many just feel that they cannot stay another day where they are now. This negative conviction may arise out of conditions that vary from liberalism to a personal disagreement with the pastor. However, if they have not grown in grace to the point where they see that the proposed mission church is needed for a positive, unique ministry, then they are not in reality seed families.

6

The Committee
on Assessment

A PLAN WHICH IS SAFEGUARDED

The outline of the procedure was given in chapter four. Its purpose is to produce self-sustaining, self-governing churches of biblical character in a relatively short time with the confidence that God's hand is on the work.

The essence of the procedure, however, is much more than to propose three mechanical steps to be more or less assured of success. The strength of the procedure first of all is the firm application of two safeguards which enable the people to be continually responsive to the Holy Spirit. The two safeguards are:

a) relating the vision and program of the work to specific scriptural goals; and

b) constantly assessing the progress towards these goals with objective, spiritual maturity.

The procedure also finds its strength in the oversight of "men of honest report, full of the Holy Ghost and wisdom," who will make the assessments demanded by these safeguards.

The method of applying the safeguards is as follows:

(1) Before the first phase is begun, those who are to be responsible for the assessment are chosen.

(2) Before each phase is begun, the scriptural goals to be accomplished in that phase are set.

(3) Before any phase can be considered finished and the next one started, the current phase must be assessed and found to be blessed by God's hand.

Those who make this assessment have three options:

(1) Proceed to the next phase.

(2) Continue in the current phase, extending the timetable and probably using additional programs.

(3) Stop the work completely.

THE PREREQUISITES FOR THE MANPOWER

These assessments must be made by men who are:
- spiritually qualified
- experienced in making decisions which are both objective and mature
- not members of the embryonic group itself.

When the significance of several interrelated conditions present in the attempt to establish a church are understood, it will become evident why these qualifications are laid down. The first of these conditions has to do with the qualifications of those making the decisions. Sooner or later some men in the group will begin to assume more and more responsibility for making the many necessary decisions. This is natural, and every effort must be made to capitalize on their dedication and abilities. However, there has not yet been enough time for it to be clearly evident that they possess the spiritual maturity which qualifies them to make the final assessment of each phase of the formula. Nor has there yet been sufficient time for the group to develop its declaration of purpose; thus there is no way to be sure these men will be well oriented to the specific purpose and consequent program of the church. Therefore the vital task of safeguarding the progress of the work must be left to men outside of the embryonic church.

A more complex condition exists if elders from other communions are among the seed families. (The problem is compounded if these elders are from a church of the same denomination.) Because of their previous ordination, there should be no question as to their spiritual fitness and ability to make decisions; yet this local group of believers should be privileged to choose for itself its own leaders. In addition to this there is the danger, because of a natural feeling of awe and respect that they may inspire as ordained men, that the rest of the seed families would be hesitant or even embarrassed to participate freely in conducting parts of worship services, drafting the declaration of purpose, proposing innovations in the programs of the church, etc. Further, although these elders may have been very well suited for leadership in another church, until the new church has developed its own declaration of purpose, it is impossible to judge their commitment to the specific purpose and consequent program of the new church. Thus it is clear that even when there are elders among the seed families, still the all-important task of assessment must be done by men outside of the group.

Another of these conditions has to do with the subjective involvement of those on the front lines of the development of the work. The degree of their involvement is directly related to their personal desire to see this attempt succeed. However, this leads to the corollary that they will experience a severe degree of anguish if they are called on to make a decision either to slow down the timetable for proceeding from one phase of the work to another or actually to stop the work. This reinforces the conclusion that the men called on to make the assessment should be men who are not in the group itself. However, they must be men who are able, as they make their assessment, to appreciate the dedication of those in the group; this again demands men of spiritual maturity.

Thus those responsible to assess the progress must be a group of men spiritually qualified, known to be objective and mature in judgment, who are not part of the group. The group will of course voice its own opinion, but the judgment of these who are external to the situation must clearly corroborate the group's conclusion that the scripture goals have indeed been met, if the decision is to have valid meaning. If their judgment does not agree, the judgment of those responsible for the assessment must be considered final.

THE SOURCE OF THE MANPOWER

The source of manpower for this task depends upon the kind of church being established. If it is part of a denominational program, the missions committee of that denomination will supply the men.

If the church to be established is to be independent, ministers and officers of similar churches could be called on to supply the manpower for the task.

Since this book is designed to be of help to both kinds of churches, the name "committee on assessment" has been coined in order to fit both situations. (Probably no committee would choose to call itself by that name, but it will suffice to designate the men throughout this book.)

If an existing independent church wants to help establish another, it will probably choose the committee on assessment from among its own officers. In the case of an individual moving to an area in which he believes a need exists for another church, he should seek the counsel and help of men of a similar church, rather than proceeding as a "loner."

The committee on assessment should have two or at the most three members.

THE TWO-FOLD TASK OF THE COMMITTEE ON ASSESSMENT

The committee on assessment will always act in the role of consultant (as that term is understood in professional circles).

The primary task it performs is to evaluate each phase in the development of the work and to determine whether or not the group should go on to the next phase.

The committee on assessment usually finds it necessary also to give counsel, primarily in the case of the independent church. These services must be rigorously guarded by the following restrictions:

- All counsel carries the weight of advice only.
- No counsel may ever be implemented directly by a member of the committee on assessment.

It has been demonstrated that when restricted by these limitations the committee on assessment can play a very necessary part in assisting the embryonic work without losing the position necessary for objectivity in its work of assessing the progress of the church.

PHASE I

7
Locating
the Seed Families

The goal for the first phase of the work is to enlist a minimum of eight to twelve seed families with whom to establish a mission church (phase two).

Seed families are families already blessed with vision, more fully described as families who:

a. are professing Christians;

b. have an apparent concern for the lost;

c. are oriented at least to the theory of the system of doctrine and form of government of the church to be established.

d. and are convinced that they must take part in establishing such a church.

The most obvious, yet most often overlooked, premise of this whole phase of operation is that a seed family may well be, and very often is, a family just recently won to Christ. If no full-time missionary is on the field to be used to reach the Lord's own with the gospel, it is often a human weakness to presume that the lost cannot be reached yet or that a family of babes in Christ could not possibly be a seed family. In all the methods to be described, never disregard this fundamental premise: the young Christian should be used for the Lord in every way possible.

It should be noted that this material does not deal with an existing particular church wishing to leave one affiliation (denomination) and become an independent church or a part of another denomination. Nor does it relate to an existing particular church which desires to multiply into two churches by using some of its own members as a nucleus for the second church. In the second case careful preparations are needed in order to have two healthy churches rather than two dead churches; these will be discussed in detail in chapter eighteen.

The methods described in this chapter are applicable if a family or several families desire to see a new church established, if a missionary settles in the area in order to be used to generate the basic core, and/or if an existing church makes a massive effort to establish a new church without using its own members. In each of these three situations, regardless of the motivation that gets the work going, the in-depth survey must be made. The methods described here can only be used when this has been done, when the data have been analyzed, and when it seems apparent that a church could well be established within reasonable time. Therefore, before phase one is begun, an estimate should be made of the time necessary to complete it.

Several methods to reach the seed families will be described in detail. Certain basic principles of application must be understood in order to make these methods of greatest possible value.

In the first place, the individual methods described may well be remodeled according to local conditions. Each of these methods has been used with a tangible degree of success, yet the conditions in location A may demand modifications and refinements not necessary in location B or C.

Next, no one method is usually successful by itself. Therefore a combination of the methods is almost always necessary.

Finally, the combination of methods implies a time schedule for one before the other or for some overlapping. Circumstances in location A may call for a different chronology of events than in location B or C.

It must be remembered that the primary emphasis of this phase of the procedure is to reach people, among whom will be the seed families. The need to engage immediately in evangelistic outreach is *absolutely mandatory*. The methods described in this chapter are not a substitute for evangelism; they are ways both to create the opportunity to practice personal evangelism and to supplement personal evangelism.

The thrust of these principles of application is that the individual or group conducting the work of establishing a new church must be very flexible as far as mechanical details are concerned. Just as important, however, is the fact that there can be little or no flexibility in the concepts underlying these methods.

Therefore each method described will be prefaced with a statement of the underlying concepts involved.

METHOD ONE: CONCENTRATED BIBLE CLASS-VISITATION PROGRAM OF DEVELOPMENT

Underlying Concepts:

1. The in-depth survey has revealed an exceptionally strong potential.
2. The committee on assessment, working on its role of offering counsel, must begin to function immediately.
3. The committee on assessment may suggest a qualified Bible teacher. The options are:

   a. In an exceptionally promising situation, especially if the underwriting finances are already on hand, the organizing pastor may be brought to the location, even at this early date;
   b. A missionary on furlough could be used;
   c. A nearby pastor could be used;
   d. Or a qualified layman could be used.

Those people directly involved must make the decision and do the arranging.

4. A definite timetable must be established at the beginning, based to a great degree on the assessment of the in-depth survey, and this timetable will be followed quite firmly unless there are extenuating circumstances which all involved agree have forced a revision of the plan.
5. A definite program of assessment must be established at the beginning.
6. Adequate preparation must be made before starting the program for the finances needed in order to carry the program out to completion.

Outline of method one:

1. Week 1:
   a. The seed family (families) are revisited. The procedure for establishing a church must be discussed in depth. The outline of this method to locate additional seed families must be presented.
   b. All necessary arrangements for the Bible class(es), including time, place, etc., should be made. It is best to have several classes each week, each one in a different neighborhood.
   c. The best means of advertising these Bible classes should be devised and the plans set in operation.
   d. Develop a referral list of contacts from each original contact and visit each new person.
   e. Leave an introductory brochure (see Appendix C) and calling card at each referral visit.
   f. Begin an extended visiting program (after referral contacts have been visited) to new houses or houses into which new families have just moved. (See chapter fifteen).
   g. Enlist the aid of as many as possible from nearby churches in this door-to-door visiting.
   h. Advertise in any religious journal (paid or free display ads), requesting the names and addresses of possible contacts in that particular geographical area who may be visited.
   i. For denominational efforts: seek to acquire names from mailing lists of mission boards, schools and colleges, agencies, etc., of the denomination, of people who may be visited.
   j. Develop a large base for prayer support, and regularly keep them informed of progress.

2. Weeks 2 through 5:
   a. Begin the Bible classes. The doctrine of the church, especially as developed in the Pastoral Epistles, is the best introductory material.
      (1) In the course of this study, stress should be laid, as the occasion arises, on the basic Christian doctrines (the inspiration of the Bible, the character of God, justification,

the responsibilities placed upon man by God, and the necessity for the existence of the church).

(2) The atmosphere of the classes should emphasize the spiritual nature of the concern for those who attend, and should give ample opportunity for questions on any subject.

(3) One of the direct values of the class to those seeking to establish a church is the opportunity to assess the spiritual stature of those attending, in order to be better prepared to decide at a later time whether or not God has provided sufficient strength to proceed into the mission church stage of development.

(4) The purpose of the Bible class should be clearly evident, although not unduly emphasized, as related to an attempt to establish a particular church in that area. Literature should be available for guests to the class, although not necessarily distributed. A clear distinction as to the ultimate goal of the class is important. Too often a Bible class is so needed in a community that it quickly fills up with those seeking to find spiritual nourishment to supplement the "starvation diet" of their own church. If, however, these people do not know the ultimate purpose of the class, they often feel misled when the fact is finally announced. On the other hand, they must be made to feel totally at home in the class, whether or not they intend to become part of the church in the future.

(5) Certain ground rules should be observed:
- Those attending should know that all questions and comments are indeed welcome and are encouraged.
- The time for starting and stopping should be determined and adhered to strictly.
- A "kaffeeklatsch" following the class is optional.
- Those attending should be encouraged to tell their friends about the class and also to give referral contacts to the teacher.

(6) Prepare a more detailed brochure (see Appendix D) to

give to families who want more data to study before becoming seed families.

(7) It is wise not to receive any offerings during the Bible class(es). If individuals request the privilege of giving, arrangements should be made personally.

b. Plan regular Sunday evening services to begin no later than the fifth week.

(1) The first of these could be in a home but would be better in a public place. The Bible classes should provide the basic nucleus and the source of word-of-mouth advertising. Public advertising could be used, but it must not be such that it would undermine the effectiveness of an extensive advertising program when morning services begin.

(2) Make the service a service of worship, not just an extension of the Bible classes. Use the best musicians available, with the minimum prerequisites that they are professing Christians, that they realize the overall purpose of that regardless of whether they would actually join the church when constituted, they are at least sympathetic to the work to be done and are not merely eager to use their talents or to be paid for services rendered. Some hymnbooks should have been ordered and should be on hand for the first service. If at all possible, do not use "leftovers" from another church; have new ones.

(3) Offerings should be received from the beginning, but should be safeguarded as outlined in chapter ten.

3. Weeks 6 through 11:

a. Follow-up work and solidification of the progress made thus far.

b. Plans to begin a morning worship service and Sunday School on or before the twelfth week should be started at least three weeks prior to the proposed date.

4. Weeks 12 through 15:

a. Begin morning worship services and probably Sunday School.

b. It must be clearly yet unobtrusively evident that this is an attempt to determine whether God will provide a sufficient number of seed families with which to constitute a mission church. Therefore it should be clear that the next stage of development is not automatically guaranteed, but that in faith the present group is seeking tangible evidence of God's blessing as a token of spiritual guidance before a final decision is made.

c. The morning worship service must be characterized by the experience of worship from the very first service. (Suggestions for order of worship are presented in Appendix A.) The temptation will be strong merely to have a make-shift service because the number in attendance is low. This must be uncompromisingly rejected. The morning worship services of the church must be of the highest quality possible from the very first. After the group becomes a mission church it will spend much time determining its particular purpose and will seek ways to express this purpose through its services of worship. Meanwhile, the morning worship services should at least include:

(1) use of all the basic parts of community worship;

(2) means for the body of believers to experience a meaningful communion with God;

(3) means for the individual believer to experience a meaningful communion with God;

(4) means for the edification of the body of believers and of the individual believers.

d. For the Sunday School, use three or four major departmental divisions if the group is small. The organizing pastor should probably teach the adults. Arrange to have teachers for each of the normal class divisions prepared to teach within three or four weeks, regardless of whether pupils exist for the classes at the moment.

e. Offerings should be received from the beginning, but should be safeguarded as outlined in chapter eleven.

5. Weeks 16 through 20:

A decision must be made on or before the twentieth week as to whether or not to establish a mission church. Four options are available:

a. Proceed to become a mission church.

b. Carry on for five to seven more weeks as at present, anticipating that a positive decision to become a mission church may well be a real possibility after that. (Note: the choice of this option must be based on specific data, not merely on wishful thinking.)

c. Arrange for a local pastor or layman to continue the mid-week Bible study and/or the Sunday evening service indefinitely, waiting on the Lord to use it for a blessing to those involved and for him to add the needed strength to go into the mission church stage when and if he clearly indicates this breakthrough. If an organizing pastor is already on the scene, this would indicate that his work, at least for the present, is finished and that he should leave.

d. Close down the operation completely.

It is mandatory that the committee on assessment be totally involved in each decision and be actually on the scene as this last decision is made.

METHOD TWO: MASSIVE VISITING AND PRESENTATION PROGRAM OF DEVELOPMENT

Underlying Concepts:

1. The key to the program is to use a great many people, in a short period of time, to present to the public the general purpose of the proposed church, and to invite them to a specific activity already functioning.

2. Two immediate objectives are to be sought:

   a. To locate possible seed families already living in the geographical area proposed, with whom to establish a mission church,

   b. and to make a telling impression on the entire area, upon which development can be based at a later date.

3. It is of maximum importance to maintain the distinction between seeking a hearing about the church and stealing members from an existing church. In every instance the task is to seek an opportunity to present the purpose, answer questions, and make it abundantly clear that any personal follow-up would be based on an

invitation from the interested party, with no compulsion involved.

4. One consequence of this effort, regardless of the number of seed families finally located, is the formation of an extensive list of families who at least have shown some degree of interest in a particular church which has this purpose in their immediate neighborhood. This becomes one of the prime sources of long-range development for the organizing pastor when he begins phase two.

5. It is very important that this method employs many people at one time and that these people should undergird their part with prayer and then, because of their personal involvement, be strong prayer supporters for each phase of the work in the future.

6. The committee on assessment will be responsible to recommend the leaders and the program necessary to enlist manpower from the sister churches for this work. The family (families) involved will do the actual soliciting of help from like-minded churches and will arrange for individuals to do the various jobs connected with this method of procedure.

Outline of method two:

1. One individual must assume the primary responsibility of oversight and direction. It could be the organizing pastor, if the circumstances are favorable (cf. Method One, Underlying Concept No. 3; Method Two, Underlying Concept No. 6).

2. Analyze the proposed region (which has been selected from the in-depth survey) in order to accomplish the task most efficiently.

   a. Analyze the region as to natural and territorial divisions, e.g., hills, valleys, major roads that divide one area from another area, subdivisions, etc., so that logical assignments of areas are made to those visiting.

   b. Select those areas which would probably offer the most immediate response and those which would offer the greatest potential for future development. Give these areas the highest priority for visiting. (For example, commercial areas and areas whose residents are very transient would be very poor neighborhoods in which to make a major effort in this program.) If there are not enough people to visit every house in the entire region, or if weather or other problems cause a change in plans, at least the areas of highest priority must be covered or the program will not be complete.

3. Distribute the workload of the visiting to be accomplished.

a. Appoint a "director of visitation" (probably the director referred to in Point 1 above).

b. The director is responsible to divide the areas of highest priority and of second highest priority into logical sections. Five sections are all that can normally be accomplished on any single day.

c. Appoint a leader for each section to work with the director.

d. Divide each section into as many "visiting sub-sections" as is necessary to cover the area. (Note: a sub-section is that which can be covered by one team in approximately 1½ hours. Its size is governed by geography and the density of houses and population.)

e. Determine the number of visitor teams (a husband and wife is the most preferable team; high school seniors are the youngest that can be used) to do the entire program of visitation in one or no more than two sessions of 1½ hours each.

4. Enlist the canvassers.

a. The director and the section leaders set the date(s) for the actual program of visitation.

b. The director of visitation must meet with at least the officers of each church willing to assist this program. The program and its details must be carefully explained, questions answered, and date(s) announced.

c. A recruiter is appointed in each church and a proposed number of visitors is assigned to that church as a quota.

d. It is suggested that the recruiting be done about two months before the date set for the visiting.

e. The recruiters give the names of each team recruited to the director; he assigns the teams to the section leaders.

f. The section leaders must train all their teams and give them their specific assignments.

5. Options for locating possible seed families by means of these visits:
   a. Option 1: Instruct each team to go into as much detail as the family visited seems interested in hearing, if the family gives evidence that it might indeed qualify as a seed family. Before leaving, a firm appointment should be made for a follow-up visit by the director or the organizing pastor.
   b. Option 2: Instruct each team to make a judgment based on the response to the initial explanation and to relay this information to the section leader. Within a few days, an appointment should be made to have qualified personnel return to these homes and present the purpose of the proposed church in depth.
   c. Option 3: Arrange for a public presentation of the purpose of the proposed church in a public building (school, motel, etc.) or for several public presentations on a smaller scale in homes. In this case, announcement is made to each family visited. From these visits a list of potential seed families, plus those that are at least interested, is constructed, and it is given to the section leader. He is then responsible that these people are reminded by telephone or mail to come to the public meeting. (See method three for details.)

6. Necessary literature for distribution by the visiting teams:
   a. an introductory brochure (see Appendix C).
   b. a brochure about the specific activity already functioning.
   c. If one or several public meetings are to be conducted, information about the time and place should be prepared for distribution.

7. Spiritual preparation for the visiting program:
   a. Weeks of special prayer sessions should be conducted by all the people involved. One of the major pitfalls of this program is a high degree of organization without prayer support.
   b. If possible, the cooperation of the pastors of the churches assisting the canvass should be sought with the suggestion that the pastor preach at least one sermon on the individual Christian's responsibility to be involved in doing the work of the Kingdom of God in his own neighborhood.
   c. A group prayer session should be conducted, about one-half

hour before the visiting teams go to their assignments, which should include the committee on assessment, the director of visitation for this program, the section leaders, the people doing the visiting, plus any others who are concerned but not able to participate in the visiting itself.

8. How to conduct the visit:

For all options: After a personal introduction by one member of the team, present the brochure and discuss in very general and brief terms the highlights of the purpose of the proposed church.

Option 1: Judge the apparent degree of interest and follow through with the approach agreed upon (see Point 5).

Option 2: Judge the apparent degree of interest and seek permission to arrange for an appointment in the near future.

Option 3: Judge the apparent degree of interest and make a record of each family showing any response.

9. Collecting the data gathered by the visitors:

a. Each team is to report back to its section leader before the end of that day.

b. The section leader must collate the results of the visits and give the director a list of every interested family (plus other specifics according to the option used) within two days.

c. The director must collate the lists of interested families into a master list and institute the necessary follow-up according to the option used.

10. The organizing pastor, if one is on the scene, or the director of the program, is responsible that all necessary follow-up of this data will be completed within three weeks. This task may have to be delegated to several qualified men.

11. Within four weeks of the visitation program the work and follow-up must be evaluated, a decision made, and all those interested notified.

METHOD THREE: PUBLIC PRESENTATION PROGRAM OF DEVELOPMENT

Underlying Concepts:

1. The greatest value of this approach is that it acquaints a large number of people with the purpose of the proposed church. Be-

cause of its public nature and because it is not a worship service, it offers the unique opportunity of inviting personal contacts without regard to their own confession of faith, position in the community, or relationship to churches of the community.

2. This meeting must be in a public building, not in a private home or a church building.

3. Under no circumstances is this meeting to have the aura of worship or any of the elements of worship (least of all sermonizing) with the one exception of prayer at the beginning.

4. All statements of doctrine and government must be based on the Bible, and the Bible must be freely and unashamedly used and declared to be the final authority for faith and practice.

5. All questions are welcomed, but this meeting is not to be a public debate and must not be allowed to become one.

6. Personal discussions with individuals must be conducted by appointment in their homes at a later time, not before the assembled group.

7. This method is usually used as a supplement to other methods. Its timing in relation to the other methods must be determined by the circumstances of each situation. Experience seems to indicate that some activity of the proposed church, at least Bible classes, ought to be already established, to which interested people can be invited. It is often wise to wait to hold the public presentation during the beginning of phase two in order to locate additional families rather than the initial seed families.

8. The speaker must be well acquainted with the distinctives of the proposed church and its consequent position on most subjects in order to answer the questions that might be asked.

9. Since this method is used in conjunction with one or more other methods, the responsibility for organizing and directing it lies on the shoulders of the director of the complementary method used or the organizing pastor himself.

Outline for Organizing a Large Public Meeting

Note: It must be clear that everything which is done is for the sole purpose of constructing a bridge of communication. If anyone wants to become part of the proposed church, he must act on his own initiative to do so.

1. Rent a post office box and a postage paid number. Rent a public meeting place for the meeting. A conference room in a Holiday Inn or Howard Johnson's is recommended.

2. Employ a telephone answering service or obtain the permission of a resident to use his phone number, possibly with an automatic answering device.

3. Place display ads (at least one-fourth page) in the local paper describing the proposed church. Include the telephone number and the post office box number. Use "throw papers" as much as possible. Two such ads are recommended for each of the two weeks preceding the week of the meeting.

4. Place display ads describing the time, place and purpose of the public meeting. Include the telephone number and the post office box number. Two such ads are recommended for the week of the meeting.

5. Use radio and/or television spots if possible.

6. If no worship service and/or Bible class is being conducted, arrange for a Bible class for at least two weeks following the public meeting. The pastoral epistles are recommended for study.

7. Distribute a letter describing the purpose of the proposed church and the purpose of the public meeting to each house in at least the highest priority area. Include the telephone number. Enclose a postage-paid card addressed to the post office box. Arrange for distribution by bulk mailing, by the members of sister churches, or by a professional distributing agency.

8. Consider each telephone and mailing response a prime contact. The organizing pastor (or well qualified people) must visit each one *before* the public meeting. The purpose of the visit is to:
   - establish a personal rapport;
   - emphasize the public meeting and urge them to attend and bring friends;
   - get referral contacts who may be visited.
   Each new referral should be visited *before* the public meeting.

9. Immediately before the public meeting, give the newspapers, radio and television stations news releases about the meeting and the speaker. Supply pictures and biographical data to the newspapers.
10. Invite reporters to attend.
11. Invite members from sister churches to attend.
12. The meeting must start on time. It should last no longer than one hour. Use as many visual aids as possible. Each guest should receive at least one piece of literature (e.g., the introductory brochure: see Appendix C).
13. Get the names and addresses of everyone present.
14. Invite everyone to the worship services and/or Bible classes.

Outline for Organizing Several Small Public Meetings

Basically the same as above, with any necessary modifications for the circumstances of a home or small public hall. This method will probably be *more* effective than the one large public meeting.

METHOD FOUR: LETTER CONTACT PROGRAM OF DEVELOPMENT

Underlying Concepts:

1. Like method three, this program is usually used as a supplement to other methods. Its timing in relation to the other methods must be determined by the circumstances of each situation. Experience seems to indicate that some activity of the proposed church (at least the Bible classes) ought to be already established, to which interested people can be invited. It is often wise to wait to do this during phase two in order to locate additional families rather than initial seed families.
2. Also as in method three, the responsibility for organizing and directing this program lies on the shoulders of the director of the complementary method used or the organizing pastor himself.

Outline of method four:

1. Locate with some degree of finality the approximate center (either geographical center or center of density of population) of the proposed outreach for the church.

2. List the names of every residential street within a given radius from the center.

3. Using the *Polk's Directory* or the *Haines' Directory* (usually available as a reference volume in every public library), address an envelope to each resident in that area. (Note: several volunteers, who bring blank envelopes to the library, could accomplish this in a few days.)

4. Mail each person an introductory brochure and a personal invitation, either:
   a. to request someone from the church to call on him in his home;
   b. or to come to a large or small public meeting;
   c. or to come to a Bible class.

5. Follow up each response as the case indicates.

METHOD FIVE: "GET ACQUAINTED OVER COFFEE"
PROGRAM OF DEVELOPMENT

Underlying Concepts:

1. This method is most effective in a neighborhood of new homes where all the residents do not yet know each other.

2. Like methods three and four, this program is usually used as a supplement to other methods. The responsibility for the program falls on the shoulders of the director of the complementary program used or of the organizing pastor himself.

3. This method permits the host to invite friends and acquaintances from quite a distance.

Outline of method five:

1. Arrange for several homes to be opened for the meetings.

2. The hosts should invite everyone they can, regardless of potentiality, but must make it clear that there will be a short presentation after the fellowship and refreshments at which time the purpose of a proposed new church will be explained.

3. The speaker should attempt to become personally acquainted with

as many present as possible during the fellowship and refreshment period. This provides him with a personal platform later.

4. The speaker should not take more than twenty-five minutes for his presentation and should use visual aids wherever possible.

5. Anyone having any interest should be listed and appointments made for in-depth follow-up conferences.

6. If any of those visited are interested enough, their homes can be used for additional sessions, so that the program can be repeated, with new contacts every time, for an unlimited number of times.

CONCLUSION

Locating a sufficient number of seed families with which to establish a mission church is often the hardest part of the total program. A few comments are in order as guidelines and encouragements in this work:

1. Time and again during this phase of the work individuals who believe that they are Christians are confronted with the true claims of Christ, and the Holy Spirit brings them to the Lord. Even one such experience more than repays the hard work done.

2. The seed families need not be elders in order to qualify; in fact, sometimes it is better if they are not.

3. No amount of enthusiasm can be substituted for a solid foundation on which to build the church. But the foundation will never be laid without the enthusiasm and confidence of those doing the work.

8

A Time for Decision:
Should a Mission Church Be Established?

The procedure for establishing a church is cemented together by the prior agreement of all involved that the progress must be safeguarded at each step of the program. In chapter five it was pointed out that those using the procedure must be courageously objective in applying the safeguards and strong enough to say *No* when the development cannot go on except by the strength of men without God.

Once phase one of the procedure for establishing a church has been instituted, it will immediately be necessary to safeguard the progress. The committee on assessment must act with clarity and dispatch to avoid either of two possible extremes:

(1) on the one hand, the attempt to locate an adequate number of seed families could drag on so long that frustration would undermine all the possible good sought to be accomplished; or,

(2) on the other hand, the seed families on the scene could get so enthusiastic that they would begin to consider themselves a mission church before an objective assessment has been made and therefore would become too emotionally involved to accept any decision except that of proceeding into phase two.

The committee on assessment, therefore, must assume its responsibility from the very beginning. This will insure an orderly, smooth course of progress into phase two and it will provide for a point of time at which a specific decision will be made. Thus conviction, not circum-

54

stances, will be in control. Needless to say, in such a situation the nature of this decision is not a simple "true or false." It must be as objective and astute as possible, but it will of necessity be a judgmental decision. The committee on assessment must assess the program in the light of the goals which have been set and then make a judgment as to the next step which should be taken.

In this assessment and judgment the committee must take into account the definition of a mission church and its implications. A mission church is:

a group of believers who, within several months to two years, seek to demonstrate both among themselves and through themselves to the world that God has indeed developed them into a self-sustaining particular church.

This definition nowhere demands that the initial seed families must have ordained elders in their midst in order to begin a mission church. Therefore, the committee on assessment must not bypass or even underestimate the potential value and service of a new-born babe in Christ when it makes its judgment. The degree of experience is not the criterion on which it bases its decision.

PREPARATION FOR THE DECISION

Assessment of the data from the in-depth survey will have indicated the minimum number of seed families needed to establish the mission church. With this minimum in mind, adequate assessment of those who could be seed families is needed. Experience has taught the lesson that the committee on assessment must visit each family in its own home and make a recommendation based on their direct contact. This point cannot be overstressed. The response from families at a public meeting (although sincere) cannot be counted as sufficient basis for proceeding.

In order that these personal visits may be meaningful and that there may be ample time for questions, several visits may be required. The visitors must be satisfied as to the following:

1. The family can make a clear-cut profession of faith. The profession is valid even if it is not expressed in standard terminology,

as long as it reflects personal salvation. Putting it another way, the family would be welcomed into any sound, evangelical church by their confession of faith. If the family does not know biblical terminology, the challenge is to the church to fulfill one of its basic functions, namely, to provide the training necessary for the babe in Christ to grow up.

2. The family has an evident burden for the lost and a desire to be used to proclaim the gospel to the lost next door as well as to the fields beyond the seas. As has been previously mentioned, these seed families have their first responsibility to their own loved ones and close friends and associates, and they cannot be hesitant or ashamed to be used to reach these people for the Lord through his proposed church.

3. The family has at least a theoretical knowledge of the system of doctrine and the form of government which will be the backbone of the proposed church. The seed family is not expected to know the minute details of either one of these facets. Also, they are probably not going to know the emotional impact of all that is involved until the work has progressed and deepened for some time. However, they must be acquainted as much as possible with the broad concepts of the proposed church.

4. The family has a definite sense of spiritual conviction that such a church should exist and that they should be part of that testimony. They must be challenged to face realistically what is ahead. This includes:

   a. blessings and benefits of establishing a mission church, including at least the following:

   (1) obedience to Scripture by being a part of the visible and the organized church;

   (2) obedience to Scripture by participating in a church which is committed to preaching and teaching that faith must relate to every facet of the individual's life, especially to the daily experience of dying to sin and living to righteousness;

   (3) obedience to Scripture by actively seeking to fulfill the

biblical obligations placed on the head of the family so that the entire family grows in the nurture of the Lord;

(4) the thrilling experience of facing the immediate challenge with so little tangible strength and consequently so much opportunity for evidence of the Lord's direct providence and blessing.

b. dangers, heartaches and trials to be anticipated, including at least the following:

(1) possible loss of half of those starting out because some families may move, some may die, and some may decide the mission church is not really what they want after all;

(2) possible ridicule for taking a stand against the established institutions;

(3) negative reaction by children who may not understand, may be ostracized by their peers, and may object to being forced into something against their wills;

(4) persecution (especially in smaller communities), often taking the form of a loss of business for the small store owners, service operators, etc.;

(5) new demands on one's time and energies that may seem out of proportion to the benefits received at the beginning.

In addition to the assessments made of the possible seed families, the committee on assessment must have specific financial information before it proceeds. In chapter ten a proposed budget will be discussed. This must be specially designed for each local circumstance, of course. However, it will provide a basis for discussion with the possible seed families to determine whether or not they have sufficient strength to undertake a work. Therefore, as each family is individually visited, the finances should be discussed, at least in general, and the family should be asked to consider before the Lord just what amount of financial help they will be able to give, if the mission church is established.

A card and a stamped envelope addressed to the committee on assessment should be left with each family. The card would be made out as follows:

I believe God would have us join in an attempt

to establish a ....

church in this area.

I shall attempt to give $ ....*per month to the*

mission church.

(Signature) ....

It is of course assumed that phase one of the procedure to establish a church would not have been started if the in-depth survey had not indicated that such a church could well develop within a reasonable time. The exact length of time needed for phase one depends on the local situation and the availability of the qualified help to do the work. However, a projection of the time necessary to complete phase one should have been made before beginning. If the time projected has elapsed and the plan has been fully carried out, but the number of qualified seed families is much too few, courage is needed to say at this time that the attempt to locate additional seed families cannot go on. Possibly the families already contacted can be provided for with a Bible class with a view towards later development. Whatever withdrawal plan is adopted, the end result must be that the work cannot go into phase two at this time.

If, as would be expected, when the time of the projection has elapsed, it is apparent that there are sufficient seed families to establish a mission church, a joint meeting of these families must be called by the committee on assessment. At that meeting the entire plan of redevelopment should again be explained, especially the anticipated blessings, hardships, cost and purpose of the proposed church. The seed families must make a corporate decision to accept the responsibilities outlined and to commit themselves to starting phase two. Then at the same meeting they will proceed to adopt the first specific plans of phase two. An outline of the initial organization to be set up at this time will be given in chapter nine.

PHASE II

9

The Mission Church:
Outline of Its Initial Organization

The decision to become a mission church (discussed in chapter eight) must be followed by specific organizational action taken at the same meeting. The committee on assessment must be prepared to present and explain the major facets of the organization and should have some proposals to make for implementing them.

The outline of this initial organization is given below. The order of the outline has been determined by experience. It reflects the order of priority in the minds of the seed families. Almost every aspect will be discussed in some depth in a later chapter. Brief comments are given here to enable the committee on assessment to handle them with dispatch.

A governing principle which must be accepted by all is this: because of the embryonic conditions of the mission church, all seed families must be prepared to relinquish one task if a more qualified individual is found, and to undertake some other responsibility in an area more suited to its own gifts.

A. *The organizing pastor.* In some instances he may already be on the scene. If not, the committee on assessment must already be considering possible candidates for the task. It is wise to have the organizing pastor arrive as soon as the mission church begins, or certainly at least within three to four weeks.* The committee on assessment should be prepared to have the pulpit supplied in the interim.

B. *The administrative committee.* This committee should be set up immediately. During this meeting many details will be brought up and referred to the committee for investigation and/or direct action.

It would be wise for the meeting to recess a few minutes in order that the administrative committee can organize itself.

C. *A temporary budget.* The terms should be adopted, subject to quarterly review the first year. The committee on assessment should be prepared with recommendations.

D. *Place and time of worship services.* The committee on assessment should be prepared with recommendations. If worship services have not yet begun, they should be started within three to four weeks.

E. *Mechanical details.*

- hymn books
- musical instruments and musicians
- lecturn
- delegated responsibilities

  —welcoming guests and ushering
  —taking and counting the offering
  —setting up and taking down folding chairs
  —advertising

F. *Borrowed elders.* The committee on assessment should be prepared to make suggestions. The men should begin serving at least within three weeks.

G. *Mission church name.* A temporary name should be chosen, with the realization that it may be changed soon. In advertising, bulletins, etc., it is necessary to indicate that this is a mission church. (This information may appear in small print under the name.)

H. *Incorporation and other legal matters.* Professional help must be employed immediately to begin to incorporate and to ascertain that any interim steps the mission church takes in this area are legal and proper.

Three additional items must be considered at this meeting. Since

---

* See Appendix B for a discussion of ways to obtain the organizing pastor.

they are not discussed in depth elsewhere in this book, they will be explained here in some detail.

I. *The Sunday School.*

1. Unless there is a large number at the very outset, it is suggested that the Sunday School be set up in four departments:

   • nursery-beginners (3 through 6 years of age)
   • primary juniors (first through sixth grades)
   • intermediate-senior (seventh grade through high school)
   • adults

2. The organizing pastor normally should teach the adult class.
3. The committee on assessment will recommend teachers for very temporary service. The recommendations should be based on knowledge gained from the reports used in the decision to establish a mission church.
4. Plans should be made to have a teacher prepared for each of these departments each week, whether or not students are anticipated.
5. A temporary Sunday School superintendent will be selected within a month or two.

J. *Advertising.* Some advertising *must* be done in public newspapers. The amount of money available will quickly determine the amount of display ad work that can be done.

Several other ways are open to the embryonic group to attract attention:

   • Have a news item in the paper: usually on the same day the *paid* display ad is run.
   • Use pictures and biographical material about any guest speakers and about the organizing pastor on his arrival.
   • Seek to have the display ad placed in an unusual part of the paper (perhaps on the sports page).
   • Use all the free advertising available to churches.
   • Use sermon titles that are relevant to the times.
   • Advertise freely in the "throw-papers" of the community.
   • Submit write-ups to the papers of every special event.

- Offer to write material for columns, etc., for the religious editor of the papers.
- Occasionally submit letters to the editors.
- Investigate any radio and television outlets in the community as a possible means for a paid spot.
- Engage in the "dialog" of the community on worthy issues and have the organizing pastor sit on the public panels, etc.
- Arrange for the organizing pastor to be involved as a clergyman and a professional of the community whenever possible in community activities.

The most effective advertising always is the personal invitation of the members to their friends and neighbors.

K. *A timetable.* Finally, a timetable must be adopted for the development and evaluation of the mission church. So often sincere Christian people look on the suggestion that the church should set goals to be achieved by a reasonable time as an indication of reliance on the flesh rather than on the Holy Spirit. The writer to the Hebrews, however, points out that his readers have not progressed at a reasonable rate:

> For when for the time ye ought to be teachers, ye have need that one teach you again which be the first principles of the oracles of God; and are become such as have need of milk, and not of strong meat" (Hebrews 5:12).

As to a timetable for development, a program might be worked out based on the following suggestions:

- Sunday School to be in operation immediately, with the basic permanent teaching staff set within four to six months.
- Membership training classes to begin immediately.
- Young people's programs to start as soon as possible, no later than four months.
- Study for the initial declaration of purpose to start within two to four months; to be complete within seven to nine months; declaration to be in final form within an additional nine to fifteen months.
- Finances: a stabilized income and expenditure within three months; income to show increase within four months.

- Outreach programs (see chapter fourteen) to be started between the first and fourth months.
- Officer training classes to begin in four to six months.
- Work on the constitution and bylaws to start in four months; to be complete in fifteen months.
- Members: a net increase of 25 to 50 percent sought within twelve months.

As to evaluation, the committee on assessment should be abreast of each development. It should program an evaluation meeting every quarter the first year and probably semi-annually for the next year.

10
The Mission Church:
Its Organizing Pastor

In chapter four the organizing pastor was defined as a teaching elder with vision. This definition was expanded to describe a man who is:

a) a qualified teaching elder;
b) concerned for the lost;
c) concerned for the growth of the Christian;
d) concerned for the blessings that come only from the interaction of families under the influence of the Holy Spirit working in the visible church;
e) willing to work with abounding energy and imagination;
f) a living communication of his vision;
g) and a man of decision and action.

There was a time when a well-intentioned, sincere Christian could have a very effective ministry as a pastor with no formal theological training. There is still a vast field of service open to such a person, but the office of organizing pastor in America today is no longer in this category. Whether one is called to minister to the inner city or the rural farm lands, the youth and young families of today are the products of television and mass education, and they have a sense of being unfulfilled in spite of material affluence and sociological change. They are asking questions, often by their actions, which demand a mind well trained in the Bible, in a system of faith based on the sovereign God and on his work in his world, and in the answers to the skeptics. The organizing pastor must be qualified in order to be effective.

The organizing pastor must have a heart for the lost. I have taken part in the examination of at least thirty young men seeking to be ordained to the ministry of the gospel. The questions about theology are often many and complex, and this is as it should be. Two questions often remain unasked, however, which are just as important:

(1) Do you have a real burden for the lost, that they might be saved?

(2) Does the Word of God "burn in your bones" so that you *must* preach?

The work of establishing a mission church is a far cry from that of conducting a scholarly discussion of the nuances of this or that tiny detail—it is a frontline battling for men!

The organizing pastor must also have a heart for the Christian. The mission church that is really healthy has an outreach for the lost, has babes in Christ who must be fed the milk of the Word, and has the more mature Christians who must be fed on the meat of the Word. It will probably have a predominance of the latter—in fact, it may seem that the mission church is "all chiefs and no Indians," since many of the "Indians" will remain on the sidelines until there is a going concern to join. Whatever the degree of spiritual maturity, the organizing pastor must feed his flock so that each member of the group is better prepared to respond to the personal work of the Holy Spirit and daily die unto sin and live unto righteousness.

It is paramount to point out that one of the ways the Holy Spirit accomplishes this goal is through his blessed ministry of fitly framing together the families of the mission church so that they are growing into the temple of the Lord. The framing together is accomplished by the interaction of each individual with God through an increasing knowledge of his Word, and also through the interaction of individuals with others in the mission church through their common commitment for the establishment of the Word. It was certainly our Lord's own promise before departing from this world that he would send the Comforter to be with as well as in the disciples. As the organizing pastor responds to the burden of his heart and becomes a tool of the Holy Spirit in this ministry of the growth of the Christian and of the church, his rewards are beyond the material benefits of his profession. If no such burden exists on his heart, the interaction spoken of above may be the source of such trial and difficulty that he will feel frustrated and defeated and will fail to accomplish his calling.

The organizing pastor must be willing to work with abounding energy and imagination. Common sense seems the only evidence necessary to convince a man that the task of the organizing pastor demands abounding energy. From the human point of view, establishing a mission church is often equivalent to starting a business from nothing. There is no escape from long hours and hard work. The people must have their share of energy, too, but theirs will soon flicker out if they are not able to see the organizing pastor going on and on energetically.

Coupled with that energy must be an imagination which is willing to try the new and unusual, which is not shackled by: "That's the way we've always done it!", yet is willingly submissive to the system of doctrine and the form of government to which the work is committed. One way to put it is to imagine that on the right is an unscalable cliff called doctrine, and on the left is another unscalable cliff called government, but in the area between these cliffs there is no limitation as to the path one may choose in going through the canyon. To get the church established may call for charting new paths as to the time of services, the way Sunday School is conducted, the order of worship of the morning or evening services or both, the proportions of funds in the budget, etc. In charting these new paths the imagination can run wild with new ideas. Each one must be thoroughly tested for its conformity to doctrine and government, but otherwise there is no limitation placed upon the imagination. The organizing pastor must be ready to propose some of these ideas himself and must learn to accept them when others think of them first.

Actually, all the characteristics mentioned thus far are basically those of any pastor and are not necessarily distinctive qualities of the organizing pastor. The remaining two qualities should be singled out as necessary for the special calling of an organizing pastor (with the frank admission that they are not always so absolutely essential for a successful pastorate in an established church). They are both God-given gifts (subject, of course, to being developed to greater usefulness) which enable him to accomplish so much in so many differing areas of the work with little apparent effort and all in a very short time. In the first place he must be a living communication of his vision. From the point of view of those who meet him, his gift has often been described by the remark: "His faith is contagious!" This use of the word "faith" means both his doctrinal stance and his personal conviction that God is working right here and now through him. From his own point of view, this gift motivates him:

- to regard every person he meets as a prospective convert for Jesus Christ;
- to regard every general contact he makes in the community as potentially another plank of the platform necessary for the church to be accepted as an integral part of the community life;
- to regard every problem as a challenge to seek new and often special blessing from God; and,
- to regard all these experiences, taken as a corporate whole, as ways by which God is daily making him a better servant of his, and daily providing him with the necessary stimulation continuously to enjoy his work to the full.

In the second place, he must be a man of decision and action. It is not a question of decisions of morality at this point but a question of activity decisions. For example: Do we start a Bible class in this neighborhood or that neighborhood, or possibly not at all at this time? To be a successful organizing pastor he must be able to make judgments regarding the future, because this is the foundation of making activity decisions.

This is an area grossly misunderstood among evangelicals and a detailed presentation is therefore necessary. For the sake of contrast, the commonly used but mistaken procedure will be discussed before the proper procedure. Too many people have the mistaken idea that activity decisions are made by gathering "all the facts" concerning a given circumstance and then studying them until the pattern of a solution becomes apparent. This is akin to fitting together the various parts of a jigsaw puzzle until the last piece falls into place. There is no question as to the sincerity of anyone proceeding this way. However, the validity of the procedure comes into grave doubt in the light of such questions as: How do you know that "all" the facts are indeed before you? How do you know all the "facts" are indeed facts and not, for instance, someone else's presumptions? How do you know that you properly understand the "facts" before you? How do you know your juggling of the facts until they apparently fit together is not unconscious coercion rather than objective deduction?

Actually the proper procedure for making decisions is to make intelligent judgments. To do this, all the available data concerning a given circumstance must of course be gathered together. Then an assessment must be made of their meaning and value. This means that an assessment must be made of the direction, degree of motion and cause for this direction and motion evidenced in related and parallel circumstances. (For instance: Have there ever been Bible classes in the neighborhood before? If so, how did they start? How well did they grow in a reasonable time? What apparently caused them to succeed or fail?) Finally, after relating together the ultimate goal for the entire work and the assessment of the meaning and value of the data surrounding the immediate circumstance, a judgment is made as to what course of action will bear the most results for the future. This is a decision on which the action will be taken.

An example of this kind of decision-making from everyday life may help demonstrate its use. In the history of the stock market, when the market falls, many people decide that they must get out and so they sell. It should be obvious, however, that others, looking at the identical sets of "facts" nonetheless decide to buy. If they did not, those wanting to sell would not have any buyers! Both decisions are activity decisions; both are in fact judgments regarding the future.

The organizing pastor must be a man who, after making a decision, can organize a means to implement his decision and will move into action to get it done. He will make mistakes, true. He may even make quite a few mistakes. However, because of his calling and training, the majority of his decisions will be workable, and this much activity will carry the work along while he is correcting the mistakes.

THE ORGANIZING PASTOR'S TASK

The task of the organizing pastor has already become somewhat clear as we have looked at the man to do the job. The task could well be summed up as the man of God's choice leading a small group of believers by faith to accomplish a God-given commission: establishing a particular church. The essence of his ministry, then, is to be a minister of the gospel, to keep the sense of vision alive, and to guide the people in the truth, while leading them away from presuming on God or living with unrealistic priorities.

First and foremost in his task is his preaching ministry. ("For after that in the wisdom of God the world by wisdom knew not God, it pleased God by the foolishness of preaching to save them that believe." I Corinthians 1:21). Although the organizing pastor will find himself doing many things during the infancy of the mission church, none will be of more importance than the messages he delivers. This ministry will bear the marks of his own personality and conviction, to be sure. However, it must:

(1) nurture the seed families so that they are growing in grace and thus becoming more able to do the task of the mission church,

(2) encourage the seed families to bring others,

(3) and be of such a caliber that the guest who comes is persuaded to return to be fed again.

In order to accomplish this his ministry must meet the following criteria:

(1) The preaching must be *Bible-centered!* Whether the sermon is topical, expository, or a running commentary; whether it is related directly to some current item of news or to a pertinent theme as developed from the Bible, it must be the BIBLE which is presented and which the hearers remember as the authority for and therefore the essence of the position of this church.

(2) The content of the sermons must stress as their cardinal points salvation by grace and a life which is so different because of that grace that it brings glory to God.

(3) The person and work of Jesus Christ ought to be a major source of sermon material in one way or another during the early stages of the mission church's experience.

(4) The preparation and presentation of the messages must reflect the culture, the academic standards, the degree of spiritual maturity and doctrinal knowledge and the emotional attitudes of the mission church so that the messages successfully communicate the truth to the hearts of the people.

(5) Each message must be an expression of conviction based on the authority of God's Word.

(6) Each message must be delivered with zeal and vitality.

(7) The context of the entire preaching ministry must be such that contemporary man is shown the challenge and fulfillment of life in Jesus Christ, God in the flesh, who relates the natural man to the supernatural God.

The Scripture still stands: "How shall they hear without a preacher ...?" Because of the pressure of life in the mission church, the primary task of the organizing pastor, the sermon preparation, both from the point of view of academic excellence and of personal spiritual preparedness to stand behind the pulpit for even a small number of people, is likely to suffer.

Most people in the church will assume responsibility in indirect proportion to the pastor's availability to do the work If he can take the time to do it, they probably will not. Yet one of the fundamental concepts is that the organizing pastor is to be used to prepare his people to be the servants of Christ one by one ("... and some pastors and teachers for the equipping of the saints for the work of service..." Ephesians 4:11-12, ASV). Therefore he must do his task if the church is to be blessed, but not feel that he must do everything or the church will fail.

During the period of establishing the mission church the organizing pastor must guide his people in drafting one of the most important documents the church will ever produce: its constitution and bylaws. This subject will be dealt with in detail in chapter thirteen. It will be sufficient at this point to mention that each church, although it may well have identical doctrinal and governmental principles with others (especially if it is in a denomination) has its own specific purpose, which will shape the constitution and bylaws of the church.

Another major task (to be dealt with in full in chapter twelve) is the institution of a membership training program and of an officers' training program.

Much thought will be given to finances and a building program during these early days. It is the organizing pastor's task to understand at least the basics of each and to be used to determine that all the principles and practices adopted are biblical. He must not do the work in the financial area, no matter how difficult it is to have someone else do it!

Of course, he must begin to establish a ministry that is recognized and appreciated by the community as a whole. This will mean much visiting, some of which will be for general purposes as well as visiting for spiritual purposes.

Finally, he must not neglect his family. It is true that one fundamental part of the organizing pastor's call is that, because he is the head of his home, his family is called with him into the ministry. God can and does give this assurance to the minister's wife and to his children too. However, because of his work load, he often neglects his family, supposing that, since God has called them into the work with him, God will also make it unnecessary for him to fulfill all his responsibilities as head of the home. The answer to the pastor's dilemma often is a radical reorganization of the work schedule. An example is:

- Private devotions and study before breakfast
- Continued study after breakfast until mid-morning
- Bible classes and hospital calls until noon or shortly thereafter
- Visiting, office detail, etc., until 4:00
- With the family from 4:00 until 7:00 p.m.
- Evening meetings, visits, study, from 7:00 p.m.
- Plus: One day each week away from the work entirely, and most of one day each week on concentrated study and sermon preparation.

Starting with himself before his Lord, the organizing pastor must be totally involved in ministering the gospel. He must constantly keep the fires of vision burning brightly and guide his people into the truth, even while leading them away from the sins of presuming on God or living with unrealistic priorities.

11
The Mission Church:
Its Principles

The mission church begins with eight to twelve seed families. During this phase of development they are under the ministry of the organizing pastor. They anticipate God's blessing on the mission and expect to demonstrate, in objective and tangible ways, that God has in fact developed the mission church into a particular church. It is expected that this development will be accomplished within a period of six months to two years.

Just as there was a necessary time for making the decision that a mission church should indeed be established, there will also be the necessity of a time for decision before this phase of development is considered to be completed. The objective evidence must be examined and evaluated to be confident that the development is of the Lord and not of the flesh. The committee on assessment, the organizing pastor and the members of the mission church must concur that God has provided this evidence.

In essence, this objective evidence that is anticipated will be found in two major areas:

(1) Internal development, i.e., that the seed families have grown in grace and zeal, that the mission church has been a blessing to their children, and that the mission church is a living, active unit, enjoying the meaning and responsibilities of the system of doctrine taught and actually using the framework of the government of the church.

(2) External usefulness, i.e., that the mission church has been used as a blessing to additional families beyond the initial seed families, especially as to salvation, and that the mission church has become aware and to some degree involved in giving to, praying for and participating in the work of the Lord through missions outside of itself. (Missions may well include Christian colleges and seminaries and specialized ministries in our own country as well as foreign mission work.)

The purpose of this phase of the procedure to establish a church is to allow six months to two years after the initial banding together of sufficient and qualified seed families before taking the step of constituting them a particular church, during which period these families have the time necessary to grow together into a particular church.

It must be admitted that this go-slow policy is often not very palatable, for it assumes that even Christian families need time to grow together before they can undertake corporate responsibilities. This fact has been proven so often by the harsh experience of small congregations, full of zeal, yet finding themselves unable to agree on a corporate decision, that it cannot be lightly dismissed or rationalized away. This harsh experience would normally be avoided by a church, regardless of its size, which had grown together enough that the wisdom of a unified congregation would be brought to bear on the decision to be made.

In order that this go-slow policy is fully understood and appreciated, the way in which a unified congregation makes corporate decisions should be explained. This explanation then will serve both as a goal to which the mission church will strive and as a standard from which comparisons can be made for the sake of evaluation. The unified congregation proceeds as follows:

- The officers either initially make a recommendation concerning a given subject, or receive a request from the members to consider the subject, after which they respond with their recommendations.
- The members consider the recommendation of the officers, often over a period of several weeks.
- The congregation then engages in a full discussion, open to all the members, so that the great variety of backgrounds, disciplines and experience would all be heard and appreciated.

- After this cross-fertilization of ideas has been accomplished and the mature judgment of the officers has been weighed in the context of the discussion, a decision is made by voting in the normal procedure.

It is self-evident that the congregation cannot be unified unless each member has respect and love for the others of the church. What is even more important, though often overlooked, is that the unity of a congregation is equally based on the members' appreciation of and agreement with the doctrine and government of the church. Needless to say, this takes time to develop. It is of course true that at no time is it the practice of a church to demand of each member total knowledge of doctrine and government; rather, every church is made up of believers growing in their knowledge and consequently in their faith. However, every church must have some in its midst who have grown sufficiently so that it can maintain stable continuity in matters of doctrine and government.

Now with this in mind it is clear that, when a group of believers have not had time to grow together, love and respect have not yet become a vital experience among the members and a stable continuity in matters of doctrine and government has not yet been achieved. Under these circumstances the discussion of a corporate problem is often distorted because of an embarrassing lack of exchanged ideas or because of ideas which are not in harmony with the doctrine or the government of the church. Another danger is that the one who speaks first, or the loudest, or in the smoothest way is followed, and a "one-man church" may be the result.

A careful study of Acts 14:20-24 shows that Paul did not place the embryonic church in Derby on its own simply because he had a group of believers together. Before "commending them to the Lord" and leaving them he had preached, taught and confirmed the believers and then ordained elders.

Still another objection to this method of slow, careful development should be mentioned. This step in the procedure indicates that the group needs to be proven before it is declared to be a permanent work in the community. It is a mission. Many feel that if a church admits the necessity of a period of probation this may frighten off the interested stranger at the very moment when he is the most needed. This position is an expression of false pride and it disregards two pertinent facts:

(1) The mission church has not been put on probation by the community to determine if it is acceptable or not, but it has placed itself on probation before God to be sure it does not lag behind or run ahead of God's hand of blessing.

(2) The mission church would not have been established in the first place if there had not been clear evidence that God's hand had already been on the group. Therefore this time of proving is an expression of spiritual maturity, not of immature insecurity.

MISSION CHURCH ORGANIZATION

An organization must be established which affords the blessings and challenges inherent in the definition of the mission church while serving as the vehicle through which the particular church will become a reality. The organization is to include:

(1) borrowed elders to take the responsibility for the spiritual oversight of the people.

(2) the organizing pastor, working with the committee on assessment, to take the responsibility for the program and policies of the church,

(3) a local administrative committee (not a "steering committee": see below) to deal with the day-by-day routine matters,

(4) and the mission church meeting regularly as a committee of the whole to evaluate the work and accept responsibilities to carry out the programs.

The fundamental design of this format is to delineate the major areas of responsibility inherent in a particular church, to separate them into natural divisions, and to assign them to qualified personnel. Then, while growing spiritually and numerically with the benefit of this provisional arrangement, the mission church will be in a position to institute the programs necessary to enable it to become a self-governing, self-sustaining particular church.

In order to put this program to work, the most important area of responsibility in a church must be the first order of business. This area is the work done by the elders. Their work has two parts: (1) to provide the spiritual oversight of the members and the church's program and developments, and (2) to establish, modify and enlarge the church's programs and departments to the end that the church is growing in outreach and in spiritual maturity. In the mission church these two responsibilities of the elders are separated. The spiritual oversight is given to elders borrowed from sister churches, and the establishing of programs and policies is given to the organizing pastor in conjunction with the committee on assessment.

The work of the borrowed elders is:

(1) to establish channels of communication with the committee on assessment;

(2) to attend worship at the mission church often enough that the borrowed elders come to know the families by name and are known by them. (This means probably a visit once or twice each month by each elder, plus one service where all will be present at least once every two months. It will also include visiting in the homes of the families);

(3) to be responsible, along with the organizing pastor, for receiving members;

(4) to deal with any spiritual problems that may arise;

(5) to assume responsible oversight for the Sunday School, youth work, etc.;

(6) to evaluate the spiritual needs of the mission church every month or two and communicate their conclusions to the organizing pastor and to the committee on assessment as a guide in planning new programs, etc.

Note: The matters of pulpit supply, basic programming, writing constitution and bylaws, etc., are primarily the responsibility of the committee on assessment.

The procedure is admittedly awkward to start and to maintain. For instance, if several of the men of the seed families of the mission church are exceptionally qualified as spiritual leaders and perhaps are even men of proven experience, the question is almost always raised: Why not use these men as the elders of the mission church?

The question must be answered, of course. Some of the principles involved have been discussed in chapter five. The scriptural prerequisites given for the office of the elder (I Timothy 5 and Titus 1) cannot be fulfilled except by this program of borrowing elders for the duration of the mission church phase.

(1) Elders should not be elected at the beginning, before the experience of life together as a church has demonstrated which men are indeed qualified. If the election takes place prematurely it usually happens that the man who speaks the most, gives the most, or does most of the work without grumbling or "parading" is elected to office. Yet none of these qualities shows that he is indeed the man for the office.

(2) In order to qualify for the office the candidate must be trained so that he comprehends the system of doctrine and form of government and is committed to accept the responsibilities of the oath of ordination. It is not enough simply to hope that he is qualified.

Furthermore, because the elders are responsible that all future church officers have the basic qualifications, and because the elders also are usually responsible for the training of future church officers, the first set of elders must themselves be fully qualified. The calibre of the future church officers is seldom higher than that of the first set of elders.

As far as this criticism is concerned, the practice of borrowing elders is admittedly awkward. But to bypass the procedure will probably undermine the future of the church.

Now because of this separation of responsibility, the other facets of the mission church organization become more clearly defined. Since the borrowed elders are limited to the spiritual oversight of the membership of the mission church, the matters of formulating policy and planning programs must be handled by others. The organizing pastor, working in direct consultation with the committee on assessment, assumes this responsibility. He must stimulate the members of the mission church to suggest new plans and refinements of existing ones; he must use his sanctified imagination, while willingly limiting himself to the church's system of doctrine and government; and he must solicit help and ideas from his advisors. New programs and policy may suddenly "leap right out of the page" at him or at the members but they should not be adopted until the mature wisdom of the committee on assessment has been duly appreciated.

The constant stream of day-by-day routine also requires that decisions be made. (For instance, should the morning service start at 10:45, 10:55 or 11:00 A.M.? Should a Christmas gift be given to the caretaker? etc.) These problems should be handled by an administrative committee, probably half men and half women, with the organizing pastor as an *ex officio* member. They are empowered to feel the pulse of the mission church and make such routine decisions on the spot. They are also charged with the responsibility to be sure everyone who shows interest is properly notified of all meetings, that the mission church itself meets often enough to be abreast of all developments, etc. It may prove advisable to have the membership of this committee rotate among all the seed families every six months during the mission church phase. The committee members should elect their own chairman, possibly vice chairman, secretary and treasurer. The matter of trustees will be discussed later in this chapter.

The mission church must meet as a congregation more often than a particular church. It will work as a committee of the whole. Its functions are:

(1) communication: to be sure everyone knows what is going on;

(2) review: to be sure that everyone understands why the programs and policies were adopted and has opportunity to express himself.

(3) educational: to go more deeply into the distinctives of the doctrine and government of the church, especially in drafting the declaration of purpose (see the discussion in chapter thirteen);

(4) advisory: to express new ideas for programs and policy to be proposed to the organizing pastor and to the committee on assessment;

(5) decision-making:

(a) specific decisions, primarily matters the administrative committee places before them;

(b) drafting of the constitution and bylaws (see chapter fourteen) and its preliminary adoption;

(c) decisions about the corporation, its trustees, properties, etc.;

(d) the firm decision that the Lord has in fact developed the mission church into a *de facto* particular church and that the mission church should be constituted a *de jure* particular church.

It should be pointed out that this plan of organization for the mission church not only avoids the concepts of the so-called "steering committee" but purposely avoids even the use of the term. Men and women have often served well and accomplished much on a steering committee. But the inherent principle of the steering committee is that these people are responsible to steer the group, which means they must assume the responsibilities of the elders. However, they have been elected to this position without consideration of training, often without sufficient consideration of qualification. Then when they attempt to do their job and become enmeshed in the detail of policy-and-decision-making, they often make the wrong decisions. Also, because of their position they are not prone to take a great deal of advice and really are not forced to, which may lead to a cleavage between them and the organizing pastor and the committee on assessment. Finally, they often find it impossible to give up the prestige of their position when it comes time to be properly constituted a church and therefore create tension, heartache, discouragement and even divisions on occasions, which the church may not outlive.

MISSION CHURCH AND DENOMINATIONAL RELATIONSHIP

If the group of seed families are concerned to be part of an existing denomination, a proper relationship must be established from the outset, whether the motivation for the church came from the denomination to the seed families or from the seed families to the denomination. It is the responsibility of the mission board of the denomination to see that this is done so that the churches geographically nearest to the mission church are not startled at the appearance of a new church near them. It is most important that the seed families fulfill all the requirements of the denomination's particular book of church order.

FINANCIAL RESPONSIBILITIES

The need to face realistically at the very outset of the work all the responsibilities and implications of raising the necessary finances for the mission church seems so apparent that a mere reference to it should suffice. Experience has shown, however, that such an assumption is not valid, regardless of the zeal exhibited by the seed families to get the work started. The subject must be thoroughly discussed, both from the aspect of the biblical motivation for giving and the specific moneys and budgets needed for the work.

Fundamental Principles for Giving

There are two biblical principles upon which all the financial programs of the church must be based. The first is that the means of raising funds must always be the reception of gifts (i.e., tithes and offerings), given in response to God's gifts of grace, love and provision for the Christian. The church should not secure its funds by means of profit-making business ventures.

Before going on to the second principle, the author feels compelled to provide at least one way of presenting this first principle to the seed families, since the concept of giving rather than earning money for church needs is totally foreign to many in the present day. It is often helpful to show a logical progression of thought that leads from a demonstration of God's goodness to the challenge that the Christian should give tithes and offerings in response to his love to us.

In the first place, the Bible clearly teaches that no man has a right to boast of what he is or has. Paul uses this argument in writing to the Corinthian church: "For who maketh thee to differ from another? and what hast thou that thou didst not receive? now if thou didst receive it, why dost thou glory, as if thou hadst not received it?" (1 Cor. 4:7). Note particularly the middle question: "and what hast thou that thou didst not receive?" Job teaches us the same truth: "Naked came I out of my mother's womb, and naked shall I return thither: the Lord gave and the Lord hath taken away; blessed be the name of the Lord" (Job 1:21). Next, we see that even the Christian was blessed by the grace of God simply because God chose to give it to him. "Herein is love, not that we loved God, but that he loved us, and sent his Son to be the propitiation for our sins" (1 John 4:10). "For by grace are ye saved through faith; and that not of yourselves: it is the gift of God: Not of works, lest any man should boast" (Eph. 2:8-9). After that, we have but to look at our daily existence in Christ to see that we do not have a right to God's constant provision as an automatic benefit or because we earn it by our good lives, but simply that God chooses to keep us: "It is of the Lord's mercies that we are not consumed, because his compassions fail not. They are new every morning: great is thy faithfulness" (Lam. 3:22-23). God's provision is given, not earned, and his grace and goodness to the Christian are given because he chooses to love us.

With this in mind we then have the spiritual insight to appreciate the impact of Paul's teaching to the Corinthian church about giving. Paul says: "Therefore, as ye abound in every thing, in faith, and utterance, and knowledge, and in all diligence, and in your love to us, see that ye abound in this grace also. I speak not by commandment, but by occasion of the forwardness of others, and to prove the sincerity of your love" (II Cor. 8:7, 8). "Wherefore shew ye to them, and before the churches, the proof of your love, and of our boasting on your behalf" (II Cor. 8:24). "For the administration of this service not only supplieth the want of the saints, but is abundant also by many thanksgivings unto God" (II Cor. 9:12). Notice that giving is described as a grace; that it is a test of the sincerity of love; that it is the means of supplying the needs of God's people and that it is the cause of great spiritual blessings in the church, all to his glory. In others words, God gave because he loved us and we, in response to his love (not in payment for it), should carry out our responsibility to maintain his work by the same means and out of the same motivation: we should give gifts out of love for the one who loves us and gives us all we have.

Finally, having established that the financial support must be given, not earned as a business profit, the extent of this giving is the question that must yet be answered. Paul teaches that it is a proportionate amount, not a fixed figure. The formula is implied in I Cor. 16:1,2: "Now concerning the collection for the saints, as I have given order to the churches of Galatia even so do ye. Upon the first day of the week let every one of you lay by him in store, as God hath prospered him, that there be no gatherings when I come." The portion is related to the extent that God has prospered the individual. This principle is, of course, the concept on which tithing is based throughout the Old Testament, and so it is logical to assume that Paul is here actually referring to tithing.

The second underlying biblical principle upon which all the financial programs of the church are based is that each member is always to be considered as a distinct individual before God and man. Consequently, every appeal to him is made on the basis that he will choose to respond to the appeal because of his personal conviction to do so. This principle is opposed to the view that the individual, upon becoming a church member, has to all intents and purposes become a depersonalized part of a mass of people who are subject to a taxable obligation to run the church. (See chapter fourteen for a discussion of the biblical foundation upon which this principle is based.)

Returning now to the financial programs of the church, a frequently used method of financing must be presented and analyzed. Often a large portion of the needed finances is given by one wealthy member or a denominational mission board in the form of gifts or grants. Although this method seems to be the best way to get a church started without undue financial struggles, and although it is usually done with the best of intentions, it can nonetheless be used by Satan to destroy the loyalty, involvement and feeling of belonging which every church member must have. Satan all too often uses this situation to foster the thought in the mind of the church member that the church has a special crutch on which to lean in a time of financial crisis. The church member often comes to the conclusion, perhaps unconsciously, that financial crises are met by pleading with men rather than by exercising faith to demonstrate the dependence of the church on the faithfulness of God. Satan usually does not stop at this point. Often the church member comes to the even worse conclusion that, in the final analysis, he is not particularly important in the church except to be present and to be counted. Hence his loyalty, involvement and feeling of belonging are often destroyed.

Before concluding this analysis, however, it must be stated that God has often used large gifts and grants. Throughout church history God often has had a small handful of men who have been both well to do in this world's goods and spiritually mature in their responsibility of stewardship over these goods. These men have given substantial gifts to the church directly and, in the last few generations, also to mission boards of the church. But they have usually demonstrated their stewardship responsibilities by refusing to become simply a source of financial dole. It is the author's practice as well as his recommendation that in this day such gifts and grants be made in one of the following ways: as matching gifts; as part of a program designed to phase out in a reasonable time; as gifts to special outreach programs (such as underwriting a missionary or a Christian education institution); or as smaller gifts to several churches rather than one large gift to one church.

A rule of thumb that is of assistance when the phaseout program is used for large gifts and grants is:

- The total amount of large gifts and grants should not be more than 30 percent of the budgeted needs of the general fund.
- The use of large gifts and grants should be phased out to nothing in no less than four years, preferably in two and one-half years.

In conclusion, the church that is careful to base its financial programs on an appeal to each church member as a distinct individual before God and man will continually enable him, whether he can give much, or little, or nothing of this world's goods, to develop the loyalty, involvement and feeling of belonging which are so needed for church unity and growth.

The Initial Budget and the Organizing Pastor's Salary

A healthy church will have its members determine that the organizing pastor's salary is adequate. However, the word "adequate" is subject to many interpretations. The fundamental principle on which a realistic figure is based is that "the laborer is worthy of his hire" (Luke 10:7). To interpret properly the term "adequate," as based on this principle, a good rule of thumb will help: The total income of the organizing pastor ought to be about the mean income of the neighborhood in which the mission church expects him to live, or about the mean of the congregation's income, whichever is higher.

In contrast to this is the rule of thumb all too often adopted by sincere Christians: Our church is to be established on faith; so our organizing pastor will be paid a minimum wage. Usually the second half of this rule of thumb is not enunciated, since it would cause a little flutter of guilt to cross the minds of the members, but it is often the unstated conclusion of the pious sounding statement, "We are establishing the church by faith." That kind of rationale could be summed up: "We are establishing the church by faith—the preacher's faith!"

To return to the proper formula, it takes into account the living standards of the people with whom the organizing pastor must deal—both the seed families themselves and those to be reached by the ministry of the church—and special conditions connected with the particular work. For instance, in order to accomplish his ministry, the organizing pastor may have to use his car a great deal more than the families of the church use theirs.

Another facet of the subject of the organizing pastor's salary is the breakdown of his salary into taxable income and allowances. The government in the United States has made this division possible as a tax shelter to the ministry. (It may well be changed at any time, of course, thus demanding a constant review of the tax situation.) One of the ground rules for making decisions in this area is: Seek to avoid, not to evade, taxes. The government does not expect anyone to pay more taxes than it legally requires, but it certainly does expect the legally assessed taxes to be paid.

Applying this concept, it is perfectly legitimate to determine a total income to be paid to the organizing pastor and then to deduct from it a reasonable amount for utilities, for car expenses (or supply a car) and for housing (or provide a house), and to declare the remaining amount of money to be the taxable income. (Other allowances could be pensions, hospitalization, etc.)

Finally, a word should be said about the advantages of the church's buying a house (manse or parsonage) versus giving the organizing pastor a rental allowance and letting him build up his own equity by the mortgage payments. One basic consideration is that the mission church may not yet be incorporated (in some states, a trusteeship), hence the collective body of people could not own property. Next, it may not be too wise to encumber the embryonic group with a mortgage when it may soon have to have a church building mortgage.

On the other hand, the church that prides itself that it is giving its pastor a side benefit by giving him a cash allowance so that he can buy his own house and build up his personal equity through his mortgage payments is often very much mistaken. Unless the pastor has sufficient capital with which to make a large down payment, monthly payments will be heavy on interest and very light on increasing equity for some years. The organizing pastor may well stay only four to seven years, in which time he really cannot build up much equity. But he personally must take the risk of trying to sell the house when he goes to another pastorate. If the market happens to be depressed and especially if he is forced to make a quick sale because of personal considerations, he may well take a major financial loss even while the congregation believes that it has given him a fringe benefit. Then, add to this picture the fact that since the property is in his name and he must therefore pay taxes on it, his possibility of making any money on the sale is probably very little.

No standard answer can be given to this question. However, there surely must be a frank and thorough discussion between the man and the mission church to reach an equitable solution before a final decision is made.

Guidelines for Tax Deduction Coverage

In today's society the legal steps necessary to guarantee that all gifts to the work will be under a tax-deductible shelter must be taken from the very beginning. Local professional assistance is absolutely necessary to assure that this is done properly. In chapter thirteen consideration will be given to a simple corporate charter. Some states (such as Virginia) do not permit a church to incorporate, but rather to declare a trusteeship, while other states may require a much more detailed document.

During phase one and possibly during the early stages of phase two, it may be necessary to have all gifts be given to an existing sister church or to the mission board and to have that church or agency return these funds to a second bank account of its own, administered with its approval by the group, in order to assure the necessary tax shelter. If this is done, certain moral restrictions must be observed:

(1) The trustees of the existing church or mission agency must be satisfied that this effort is consistent with their own charter.

(2) The trustees of the existing church or mission agency must be ultimately responsible that the use of these funds is in conformity to the legal restrictions placed on such tax shelters. For instance, they must be responsible that no one is giving with designations for the personal use of any individual, such as the organizing pastor.

(3) The donors must agree that, if something unforeseen does happen to abort the work, none of the funds given can be returned to them.

Principal Designations for Funds Received

A practical division of funds is necessary for proper handling of the moneys and for easy use in giving reports and providing an incentive for giving. The divisions are: the general fund, the mission fund, and the building fund.

The General Fund. This fund is used for the support of the mission church program. It therefore includes the organizing pastor's salary and allowances, advertising, printed materials, probably the rental for the Sunday meeting place (this could be handled through the building fund) and miscellaneous items.

The Mission Fund. This fund is used for the support of missionary and Christian education work in which the mission church has an interest. It is not used for the mission church itself.

Note that the term "benevolence fund" has not been suggested. In many people's minds this term is associated with gifts from their own possessions given on their own initiative, rather than gifts returned to God from that which he gave in the first place. Consequently, all too often the use of the term "benevolence" tends to stimulate giving which has the aura of personal pride attached to it. (Evangelical Christians are guilty of this over and over again. It is the author's opinion that personal pride, so opposed from evangelical pulpits, is flaunted in God's face in many of these same churches by their giving to "benevolences.")

The work of missions is a biblical imperative, to which the church is expected to respond with willing obedience and with an attitude of sincere thankfulness for his gifts to his child. Malachi (chapter 3) certainly teaches this truth. The Lord also made it abundantly clear in his declaration: "But when he saw the multitudes, he was moved with compassion on them, because they fainted, and were scattered abroad, as sheep having no shepherd. Then saith he unto his disciples, The harvest truly is plenteous, but the labourers are few; Pray ye therefore the Lord of the harvest, that he will send forth labourers into his harvest" (Matthew 9:36-38). Paul makes an amazing connection of thought in I Corinthians 15:58 and 16:1-2: "Therefore, my beloved brethren, be ye stedfast, unmovable, always abounding in the work of the Lord, forasmuch as ye know that your labour is not in vain in the Lord. Now concerning the collection for the saints, as I have given order to the churches of Galatia, even so do ye. Upon the first day of the week let every one of you lay by him in store, as God hath prospered him, that there be no gatherings when I come." He also emphasizes this truth by such verses as: "Every man according as he purposeth in his heart, so let him give; not grudgingly, or of necessity: for God loveth a cheerful giver" (II Corinthians 9:7), and "Thanks be unto God for his unspeakable gift" (II Corinthians 9:15).

A fear often expressed by the tiny, struggling mission church is that it cannot yet afford to give to others. This fear is not only groundless and defenseless in the light of God's plan; it is actually one of Satan's most effective tools ultimately to destroy the work. To yield to this fear in effect starts the mission church on the road of depending on self rather than faith. It will actually cause the work to dry up on the vine.

However, the distinction between faith and presumption must be maintained in the matter of giving to missions as well as in every other area of the church's life and growth. A practical procedure is to give 2 or 3 percent of all undesignated gifts to missions for the first year. This means that the mission fund will receive moneys from two sources: designated gifts to go to missions through the mission church, and 2 or 3 percent of all undesignated gifts received.

At the very outset a program of expansion should be adopted. A workable procedure is to increase the percentage of undesignated gifts to go to missions by 1 percent per year for three years and 2 percent per year thereafter until at least 10 percent of all undesignated gifts are going to missions.

A further word must be given because of future misunderstandings that could arise from the procedure. The various organizations of the church, when established (such as the Sunday School, the missionary society, the young people's groups, etc.) may well have missionary obligations of their own. These mission funds should be in addition to the church's mission fund.

The Building Fund. This fund is used for the purchase of land and the erection of a church building for the mission church. It should be established immediately. Regular designations on a percentage basis may be impossible at the very outset, but special gifts and inheritances will often be forthcoming so long as a fund exists to which they may be given. In the future, of course, this fund will be of major importance to the church.

An Overruling Principle Concerning Finances

The seed families must recognize from the beginning their responsibility to underwrite the mission church by their tithes and offerings. One absolute and unchangeable principle involved in giving is that it must be done in a regular and consistent manner. It is more important that moneys be faithfully given than that the giving be motivated by emotional appeals. For instance, if a bank is asked to consider a loan for a building program, it will look at the amount of money in the account but will also look to see that those supporting the work have done it faithfully and consistently (even during the summer vacation time) as an indication of the degree of involvement of the members.

12
The Mission Church: Its Goals

The mission church is a group of seed families who are worshiping together as a church and anticipate within six months to two years such objective evidence as is necessary to demonstrate that God has in fact developed the mission church into a particular church. Therefore, the ultimate goal of the mission church phase is to demonstrate that this objective evidence exists.

OBJECTIVE EVIDENCE OF GOD'S BLESSINGS:
INTERNAL GROWTH IN CHRIST

It has been previously stated that these objective evidences must be both internal and external in nature. As to internal blessings from God, they must produce the evidence that the seed families have grown in grace and zeal, that the mission church has been a blessing to their children, and that the mission church is a living, active unit, enjoying the meaning and responsibilities of the system of doctrine taught and the use of the precepts of the government of the church.

These evidences of the work of the Holy Spirit in the midst of the group of believers do not "just happen," nor do they develop from the enthusiasm resulting because new people are reached. They demonstate that the believers have grown in obedience and knowledge, that they have been edified through the experience of being part of the mission church.

The major specific areas where these blessings must be experienced are:

- a vital prayer life for the group
- meaningful worship of God
- an ever increasing application of doctrine in the personal lives of the members
- sincere Christian love for each other
- evidence of spiritually qualified elders, properly trained to assume the responsibility of spiritual oversight
- drafting of meaningful declaration of purpose and constitution and bylaws
- evidence of meaningful progress, derived from regular evaluation and planning sessions

1. A Vital Prayer Life for the Group

It is not by accident that this is the first item on the list of specific areas where the good hand of God must be evident. Throughout this entire program of establishing a church the fulfillment of the church's responsibilities before God demands that it actively maintain the proper relationship between the mechanics of the programs and their spiritual goals. Logical and practical planning is useless unless it is undergirded with prayer.

In order to emphasize the need for spiritual power, but to relate it to the organizational work of the church, it is necessary to recognize that the New Testament stresses the need for both together. Too many sincere evangelicals are openly skeptical of the use of anything but the spiritual power of prayer, disdaining those who would also approach the work by use of logical, practical programs. (On the periphery of the evangelical movement, or beyond, there are even those who want to substitute the practice of sharing experiences for praying together.)

If the work of establishing a church were to be attempted solely by praying, without also organizing and planning, the best that could result would be a sincere but totally unstable community destined to fragment over the shock wave of trials that come to each church. It must be immediately pointed out, however, that the opposite is also true. If the work of establishing a church were to be attempted solely on the basis of logical, practical organization, without being empowered by prayer, the best that could result would be an institution, not a living church.

The place to start, then, is with prayer. Step by step, prayer must undergird and energize the organizational work. As stated above, this relationship is stressed in the New Testament. For instance, in epistle after epistle, Paul writes of his own concern much as he does in his letter to the church at Thessalonica: "We give thanks to God always for you all, making mention of you in our prayers" (I Thessalonians 1:2). He further instructs them, concerning themselves both as individuals and as a corporate whole: "Pray without ceasing" (I Thessalonians 5:17). He specifically charges Timothy: "I exhort therefore, that, first of all, supplications, prayers, intercessions, and giving of thanks, be made for all men" (I Timothy 2:1). Yet he admonishes the churches to "let all things be done decently and in order" (I Corinthians 14:40). Further, he directs Titus: "For this cause left I thee in Crete, that thou shouldest set in order the things that are wanting, and ordain elders in every city, as I had appointed thee" (Titus 1:5); and: "But speak thou the things which become sound doctrine . . . These things speak, and exhort, and rebuke with all authority. Let no man despise thee" (Titus 2:1,15).

Just what is meant by a "vital prayer life for the group"? (Here it is assumed that the personal prayer life of each individual is also very real.) The prayer meeting of the mission church must become the "upper room" to the families of the church. Acts 1:4a teaches us that it was there that they "all continued with one accord in prayer and supplication . . ." Whether the prayer meeting is structured along conventional lines or is quite different, it must involve all the families of the mission church. Through the continual experience of praying together the power of God within and through the church becomes evident in these ways:

- Each member comes to appreciate how precious the others of the mission church find God's love, as evidenced through their lives, and thus the faith of each is deepened.

- Each comes to appreciate the steadfastness of the others of the mission church and consequently develops confidence in them.
- Each is increasingly free to share his blessings and concerns with the others of the mission church for the glory of God and the strengthening of all involved.
- The congregation places itself before God as a composite whole and anticipates that the Holy Spirit will perform his work of establishing the church as a spiritual unit by bonding each member to the others with mutual love and concern.

In the beginning days of a mission church, every week brings new victories and new problems. The prayer life of the group is the only source of power with which to cope with the heady wine of the victories and the nagging fears caused by the problems. It is in the prayer meeting that the families will be kept united and will grasp the opportunity to plead for God's continued grace. No matter how successful phase two seems to be, if the prayer life of the mission church is not the vital heartbeat of all else, the yellow light of warning must be seen— the standards for the spiritual life have not been satisfied.

2. Meaningful Worship of God

God created man a spiritual being as well as a material being. A full and satisfying life demands that the spiritual man be fed. This is partly done through private devotions, but community worship is also needed. ("Not forsaking the assembling of ourselves together, as the manner of some is . . ." Hebrews 10:25).

The mission church must provide such meaningful worship that it affords that particular blessing which can only be derived by the Christian as he worships in community with other Christians. (A more complete discussion of the worship services themselves will be given in chapter thirteen.)

3. Increasing Application of Doctrine in Personal Lives

Acts 4:13 demonstrates the meaning of this. "Now when they saw the boldness of Peter and John, and perceived that they were unlearned and ignorant men, they marveled; and they took knowledge of them, that they had been with Jesus." The fact that Peter and John had been previously unlearned, whereas now they were able to express themselves with power, indicates much more than only a spiritual stamina. Paul's words to the Romans also make it clear that the Christian must know something of doctrine and its application: "... be ye *transformed* by the *renewing* of your minds ..."(Romans 12:2).

To accomplish this renewing demands a never-ending effort by the pastor—teaching and applying the doctrines of the Bible as the source from which principles of life are derived and on which commitments of life are based. A synthesized system, at least of the basic fundamentals, is needed as the doctrinal foundation for the members if they are to gain the most from the pastor's teaching of doctrinal truth week after week. It is necessary, therefore, for all who would seek to become members to have these fundamentals presented to them. Consequently, from the very beginning of the mission church the organizing pastor must conduct some kind of introductory classes for potential members. These classes may be held with individuals or groups and should include:

(1) a survey of the system of doctrine held by the mission church;
(2) sufficient emphasis on the person and work of Christ to ensure that the gospel is actually communicated;
(3) an introduction to the key aspects of the government of the mission church;
(4) explicit data about the local mission church which is necessary for the integration of any individual into the work. (This would be a survey of the current financial situation and obligations of the mission church and of its programs.)

It must be pointed out at this time that classes such as these do not take the place of the personal testimony of the saving grace of God on behalf of each individual who desires to become a member; they do not take the place of the expression of willingness to acknowledge Jesus Christ as the Lord of the individual, personal life; nor do they imply that the prerequisite to membership is a knowledge of the entire system of doctrine held by the church or of agreement to every fine point of that system of doctrine. (It should be pointed out that such detailed commitments are made by those who will accept the office of elder or deacon, but not by the individual seeking membership in the church.)

The preaching of God's Word and the teaching of it in Sunday School and Bible classes must bear the fruit of adding knowledge to the foundation given in the introductory classes and the regular teaching ministry of the organizing pastor.

Finally, the Holy Spirit must use this knowledge to develop the fear of the Lord in the hearts of the people ("The fear of the Lord is the beginning of knowledge . . ." Proverbs 1:7). This will become apparent when individual after individual evidences that the preaching and teaching of the mission church has caused him to wage a personal war within himself. ("Walk in the Spirit, and ye shall not fulfill the lust of the flesh. For the flesh lusteth [warreth] against the Spirit, and the Spirit against the flesh: and these are contrary the one to the other: so that ye cannot do the things that ye would" [Galatians 5:16,17]). When individual after individual is daily dying unto sin and living unto righteousness, it is objectively evident that God is blessing.

4. Sincere Christian Love for Each Other

This area of blessing starts in the vital prayer life of the group. It must go beyond this, however. In the development of this grace, social activities have a role to play, but they are only a small factor contributing to the intangible yet very real experience of mutual love for each other. The major force bringing about the development of this love is the conviction on the part of each family that all the families in the mission church are willing to give of themselves for the benefit of any family in need.

At least several considerations will always be active when the grace of love is present:

(1)   Each family will have become so much a part of the body of the church that they unconsciously will have withdrawn any facade normally felt necessary in order to be accepted. They will show themselves as they really are, without fear of being relegated to "second class citizenship" by the others because they do not conform to some unwritten code.

(2)   Each family will feel so much concern for the others that they

will take the time necessary to learn about them in some detail and to pray for them specifically by family and name.

(3) All families will have developed sufficient freedom together in the Lord that there will be a natural response to the joys and hardships experienced by each family. In some instances this could be by way of actually giving or being willing to receive physical or financial help. It certainly will include the freedom of unrestrained expression to each other at times of crisis.

The Apostle John gives the ultimate illustration of and motivation for love at work: "Herein is love, not that we loved God, but that he loved us, and sent his Son to be the propitiation for our sins" (I John 4:10). He loved us when we were unlovable, and he did it without regard to our merits. He did not wait for us to reach for him (we never could in our own strength, of course); he reached for us. We are important to God. This gracious love must motivate the members of the mission church to love each other if they are to know God wants the work to continue.

5. Evidence of Spiritually Qualified Elders, Properly Trained to Assume the Responsibility of Spiritual Oversight

The mission church must have men ready to serve as elders before it can assume the responsibilities of a particular church. It is during the mission church phase that the potential elders are prepared for ordination. This preparation has the most far-reaching consequences of any part of the mission church phase.

In order to emphasize the importance of this, and to place it in a total perspective, a commonly asked question must be stated and its answer examined. The question is: "How do you know that in 5, 10, or 15 years this mission church will not be as far from the truth as many established churches of today already are?" The answer to this question has two parts:

(1) There is no way to give a guarantee that the church will never fall away; but,

(2) if the work is developed only by means that are scriptural, the seed of apostasy will not germinate. The scriptural grounds for

this answer are: "For this cause left I thee in Crete, that thou shouldest set in order the things that are wanting, and ordain elders in every city, as I had appointed thee: If any be blameless, the husband of one wife, having faithful children not accused of riot or unruly. For a bishop must be blameless, as the steward of God; not selfwilled, not soon angry, not given to wine, no striker, not given to filthy lucre; But a lover of hospitality, a lover of good men, sober, just, holy, temperate; Holding fast the faithful word as he hath been taught, that he may be able by sound doctrine both to exhort and to convince the gainsayers" (Titus 1:5-9; cf. I Timothy 3:1-7). In analyzing these passages of Scripture, two aspects stand out:

a. the specific fact of the actual statements themselves, which are worthy of much study, but which are not the major point of this analysis; and

b. the underlying principles upon which these statements stand. These underlying principles can be summarized in three statements:

1. things were *first* put in order in each city;

2. *then* qualified men were ordained as elders; therefore,

3. these men must have been qualified *before* their ordination.

From this analysis it is evident that the matter of qualification is of major importance. A study of these passages, coupled with a study of the apostolic church at work as revealed in the New Testament, imply that those who are to be considered as qualified possess several distinguishing characteristics:

• They are already spiritually mature men of God.

• They are already well acquainted with God's Word and are in the practice of teaching it and defending it.

• They are already administering Christian discipline as a way of life in their own families.

They must also possess an additional characteristic, although it does not in itself set them apart as do the first three:

- They are willing to take the time necessary in order to do the work involved in the office.

In other words: The potential elder is already qualified for the office; conferring the title on the man does not qualify him.

As explained in chapter eleven, the mission church does not have its own elders. When the mission church is constituted a particular church, men from the congregation will be elected, ordained and installed as elders. During the mission church phase, the organizing pastor will be preparing men for that office.

One of the consequent problems the organizing pastor must face is that of conducting nominations for the office of elder in an embryonic group which does not yet have bylaws to govern the procedure and does not yet have a firm membership list to qualify the voting. Therefore the best course of action is to invite all the men 21 and older to participate in an eldership training program. The training will be beneficial for all. Everyone taking the work must be aware that completion of this training is not to be construed as tantamount to being nominated for election.

When the mission church is ready to be constituted a particular church, the committee on assessment will decide which men will be nominees for the first election of the particular church (the details of this procedure will be discussed in chapter seventeen). If there is a real love for one another developing, the families involved will not feel disappointed or ashamed in any way if the man of the house is not nominated at the conclusion of the training period.

The training program conducted by the organizing pastor must include several basic factors:

(1) Each man must read the theological and governmental documents of the church, or those suggested by the committee on assessment, during the time when the training classes are being conducted.

(2) The organizing pastor must teach:
   (a) the scriptural qualifications for the office of elder;
   (b) the key points of the system of doctrine of the proposed particular church;

(c) the key points to the government of the proposed particular church;

(d) the responsibilities especially involved in the office of elder;

(e) the programs now used and those envisioned for the proposed particular church in its outreach to the lost;

(f) at least a sketchy survey of some of the major religious developments in the country and throughout the world.

It is the responsibility of the organizing pastor that he has actually communicated with the men and that they not only can recite "the answers" but that they have been challenged to weigh the material taught and truly believe it and are prepared, if elected, to accept all the implications of taking a holy oath of fidelity to their convictions.

6. Drafting a Meaningful Declaration of Specific Purpose and Constitution and Bylaws

This is a major area of work during the mission church period. Since it must be discussed in complete detail the title for the material is merely included at this point in order to indicate its logical relationship to the subject matter of this chapter; the next chapters are entirely devoted to these documents.

7. Evidence of Meaningful Progress, Derived from Regular Evaluation and Planning Sessions

Regular congregational meetings must be held (probably one every quarter for the first year) to evaluate progress, to make necessary adjustments in existing programs, and to plan for the future. The committee on assessment must be involved in each of these meetings, and it is from these meetings that the committee will garner its conviction as to whether the mission church is indeed becoming, *de facto,* a particular church or whether it is standing still or even falling apart.

It has been previously pointed out that the mission church must meet more often in congregational meetings than does the particular church, and that it normally will work as a committee of the whole. The various functions of these meetings were explained in chapter ten.

During the course of accomplishing these functions, the committee on assessment, the organizing pastor, and the members of the mission church will each be seeking the conviction that good and sufficient progress is being made toward accomplishing the major goal of the church—i.e., bringing glory to God through the preaching of the gospel to the lost and through the building up of the Christians in Christ.

It is in these sessions that each of the activities of the mission church, including the work of the organizing pastor, the work of the members themselves and the programs of the church, are discussed to determine if God is indeed blessing, and if these activities and programs are indeed each oriented toward the ultimate purpose of the church.

Also, it is in these sessions that the stress on the value of the individual is assessed, to be sure that the individual is not being sacrificed for the sake of so-called efficiency.

Finally, in these sessions an assessment must be made of the degree to which suggestions and constructive criticisms previously agreed upon have been applied. This particular assessment is made in every area under discussion. However, although many subjects may be introduced at one session and not another (such as drafts of the constitution and bylaws), certain subjects must be treated in every evaluation session. They are:

(1) relationship of all activities to the particular purpose of the church and to the individual policies and principles motivating them;

(2) finances;

(3) effectiveness of present programs;

(4) degree of involvement of all the members;

(5) new ideas and new programs.

The assessment of subsequent developments from plans in operation, and from suggestions and constructive criticism in these five areas is the major source of conviction as to whether or not God is developing the mission church into a particular church.

OBJECTIVE EVIDENCE OF GOD'S BLESSINGS: EXTERNAL GROWTH

The external blessings from God must produce the evidence that the existence of the mission church has been a source of spiritual blessing

to more than the original seed families. The evaluation of these circumstances is an easier task than that of the internal blessings previously
described. Three major areas of God's work must be evaluated as to
external blessings:

- By the time a mission church is ready to become a particular
church, at least a few new families must be involved in the work.
It is hoped that some of these have become Christians through
the ministry of the mission church. Many of them must have
become the equivalent of additional seed families by the time an
assessment is made.

- The mission church must be recognized as a part of the community. In some cases specific activities for service in behalf of
the community will not yet have become available to the mission
church. However, its reputation in the community will have been
developed to some degree and this reputation must be assessed.
If the business, the cultural, the educational and/or the social
segments of the community do not even know the mission church
exists or have justifiable criticism of its reputation in the community, there is a grave question as to whether or not God is
developing this work into a particular church. Note: The community's reaction to the gospel should not be confused with its
reaction to foolish or unnecessary church activities, such as using
private parking facilities without first asking permission.

- The mission church must have become involved in missions outside
itself. One of the harsh facts of reality is that a church concerned
only for itself is unbiblical and is doomed to spiritual failure even
if it is able to pay all its own bills. The seed families, then, must
have some personal acquaintance with some missionaries, be committed to praying for them, and be involved to some degree with
a regular financial support program.

CONCLUSION

The goals presented here are not elusive or unrealistic. They are
objective accomplishments, capable of evaluation. The mission church

should know what they are and recognize that the major purpose of existing as a mission church is to grow in such a way that it cannot be denied that God is developing this work into a particular church.

The options open to the committee on assessment, however, cannot be ignored. Over and over it must be restated that existence as a mission church is no guarantee that a particular church must develop. If the committee on assessment cannot honestly declare that God is blessing the work, it must reschedule or stop the work altogether.

13
The Mission Church:
Its Declaration of Purpose

In chapter three we discussed the impression the community receives of a church. By way of review, it seems in order to restate the principles expressed in that chapter. First, there are five factors which influence the outsiders' opinion of the particular church: the worship, the people, the programs, the building(s), and the ultimate size. Whether the observer sees only one of these factors or studies carefully all five of them, it is from these impressions that he draws his conclusions as to what kinds of people make up the church and what concern they have for their God and for the non-member.

Second, the declaration of specific purpose is based on a consensus of opinion that demonstrates what expression of the five factors of influence:

- most fulfills the members;
- most adequately demonstrates what concern the church member has for his God and for the non-member;
- and most successfully serves as a meaningful communication to the community which the church anticipates reaching.

The declaration of specific purpose is, in fact, the way in which the local church applies the universal purpose of the church to its own life.* Finally, the declaration of specific purpose adopted by the particular

---

* Refer to chapter 3.

church is most meaningful when it is based on the commitment to those approaches to church life and outreach which will best achieve the purpose.

PROCEDURE FOR PREPARING THE DECLARATION OF SPECIFIC PURPOSE

The task of preparing a declaration of specific purpose is exceedingly difficult. It must be understood from the outset that the declaration is to be limited to an expression of that point of view of the seed families which they are convinced before God should govern the entire life of the church, thus giving the church reason to exist in the first place. The steps necessary to prepare the declaration of specific purpose with which a church will operate usually take at least six months to complete, and could take 18 to 24 months. The following discussion will outline the procedure involved.

(1) At the very outset, the seed families and the organizing pastor will prepare an initial declaration of specific purpose. It will be theoretical, of course. It will express the burden on the hearts of the people for the direction of this church. It must be adopted along with a commitment to be ready and willing to refine it as many times as seems necessary during the mission church phase. (Note: by "refine" is meant to make the basic philosophy more comprehensive, more understandable, and related more practically to the life of the church. It does not mean to change the philosophy of church life expressed originally. Only after much prayer and deliberation should such a change be made.)

(2) The principles of the initial declaration of specific purpose must be applied to every aspect of the life of the church from the outset. During the regular evaluation and planning sessions the initial declaration of specific purpose must be evaluated to determine its relevance to the everyday life of the church, and consequent refinements must be made.

(3) Preliminary work on the first draft of a constitution and bylaws should be started within four months after the mission church begins to function. These must be in accordance with the declaration of specific purpose. As considerations of the details of the

constitution and bylaws in turn reflect on the practicability of the declaration of specific purpose, the declaration must be continually made more specific.

(4) After the constitution and bylaws are agreed upon by the mission church, the declaration of specific purpose must be put in its final form and inserted into the constitution.

PRELIMINARY STUDY: DETERMINING THE EXISTING CONDITIONS

A preliminary analysis must be made of four subjects, each of which will have a direct bearing on intrinsic opportunities and limitations already existing in the minds of and/or circumstances surrounding the members of the mission church. These subjects are:

(1) *The previous church experiences of the seed families.* The members of the mission church must assess the value of any previous church experiences for themselves and their children. They must be sufficiently objective so that sentimental attachments to men, services, procedures and family do not unduly influence their evaluation as to whether or not the actual purpose of the church was tangibly achieved. The analysis will prove to be difficult to write down, but it is necessary at least to undertake the study in order to give each member of the mission church a point of reference with which to compare the meaningfulness of the initial declaration of purpose when it is finally completed and also on the basis of which to evaluate whether the mission church is actually getting across the impression it wants to in the months ahead.

Since it will prove very difficult to reduce to writing and since it will eventually become quite personal for each member of the mission church, it is wise to start this phase of the analysis in a very general way, acting as a committee of the whole, in order to assist everyone to comprehend what is to be done, but then to have each family work up its own conclusions individually. The results need not be culled together. Experience shows that they will be the basis of contributions to future discussions and thus will adequately influence group decisions without the need of divulging the personal details.

(2) *The churches already in· the community.* Analysis of the data from the in-depth survey concerning churches already in the community (see chapter four) is mandatory. A guideline for this analysis must be stressed: never take it for granted that all churches using the same name are actually the same; take the time to know each church individually.

(3) *The neighborhood itself* (e.g., its general and commercial make-up; its history; its growth patterns; its religious make-up; etc.). The study almost always proves a revelation to a new church. The results of the survey, made before the decision to establish a mission church was reached, will be the major source of data for the study.

(4) *The communities the mission church anticipates reaching for Christ.* "Community" is usually understood as a synonym for "neighborhood," a group of homes set apart by some kind of boundaries, usually geographical.* It may be that the common denominator of living is an ethnic background, but this circumstance is not nearly as prevalent as it was a few years ago, and it has far less value to church life in America today than it did a generation or two ago. More often, the common denominator is a cultural quality, such as a common interest in the arts, or a mental attitude, such as a desire to understand thoroughly the whys and wherefores of any proposal before accepting it, or a predisposition toward a system of thought, such as a disposal to a centralized form of local, state and national governments. In this definition of "community," ethnic, educational, racial and financial differences are usually of little significance. The "community," as understood in this sense, is the foundation for friendships of everyday life. It is on the basis of this definition that this analysis must be made.

The geographical area proposed for the location of the mission church will almost always include several such communities. The study of "community" will therefore be used to answer the following questions:

---

* See Definitions, p..viii

What is the common denominator of each of the major communities of the proposed area?

What specific use of the five factors of influence (worship, individual lives, programs, building, ultimate size) will most effectively communicate the specific purpose of the church to communities?

DRAFTING THE DECLARATION OF SPECIFIC PURPOSE

From the preparatory study most of the opportunities and limitations which will shape the declaration of specific purpose will have become apparent. Now within these boundaries each of the five factors of influence must be analyzed, individually and then collectively, in order to construct the declaration of specific purpose. This analysis must reflect several mechanical precautions:

(1) The definition already given in chapter 2 of the particular church is, of course, an expression of why a church exists as well as merely a statement of what it is. The declaration of specific purpose, in beginning with the specific purpose of this church, is in no respect to be an alteration of the definition given. It is a statement which expresses how a local body of God's people believe their church should conduct itself so that it is both a truly biblical church and the most relevant possible church for their specific community.

(2) Care must be taken that each major concept is expressed as a statement of principle; these statements must be expressed in such a way that they are easily comprehended and that they are indeed practical.

(3) Care must be taken that there are sufficient data and illustrations used to make these principles of relevant use for future study.

(4) Care must be taken that the data and illustrations presented simply illuminate the principle and do not appear legalistic.

COMMENTS TO ASSIST
IN THE ANALYSIS OF THE FACTORS OF INFLUENCE

(1) *Worship.* Webster's Unabridged Dictionary defines *worship* as follows: (as a verb) "to adore or pay divine homage to God"; (as a noun) "a prayer, church service, or other rite showing reverence or devotion for a deity . . . religious homage or veneration."

The Christian must worship God. In his worship, whether public or private, the Christian's total being seeks to adore God in response to his grace. While the worshiper is thus glorifying him, God in turn blesses him by fulfilling his spiritual being. This blessing carries with it the additional benefit of making it a joy for the Christian to live in obedience to him.

This understanding of worship will provide the basis for the discussion which the mission church must conduct in its analysis of this factor of influence.

Experience indicates that the mission church may find the discussion of its worship services subject to several dangers. The discussion may produce a division of thought as to the degree of formality and liturgy to be used or it may produce an order of worship from which no deviation is allowed. These dangers must of course be overcome. As to the second one, a comment is in order. Such rigidity will destroy the very blessings it was designed to protect and therefore should be avoided.

To analyze this factor of influence systematically, at least the following topics must be discussed:

- the designation of the stated services of the church and the time each should begin;
- the very purpose of worship itself;
- the order of worship*;
- the place in the order of worship for the sermon and the purpose of the sermon;
- the kinds of sermons to be delivered;
- the kinds of music to be used (i.e., the variety, the quality and the quantity of hymns, special music, etc.);
- spontaneous prayer;
- new methods of worship.

No additional comments are needed about this list of topics except for the last one: new methods of worship. In today's world, meaningful methods of worship must be devised and used so that the worship

---

* See Appendix A for several examples of order of worship.

is relevant to contemporary life and its pressures. As such, they may be new to the church. Such methods may seem to be too daring to some members who are oriented to very traditional practices. Although these people must be respected and taught, still the attempt to devise and use new methods must not be abandoned.

Biblical standards must be used both in devising new methods of worship and in evaluating any suggested methods. The Westminster divines rightly expressed the standards to be used. They wrote:

> But the acceptable way of worshipping the true God is instituted by Himself, and so limited by His own revealed will, that He may not be worshipped according to the imaginations and devices of men, or the suggestions of Satan, under any visible representation, or any other way not prescribed in the holy Scripture. Religious worship is to be given to God, the Father, the Son, and the Holy Ghost, and to Him alone . . . *

The major thrusts of this quotation are the principles to which every method of worship must conform:

(1) Acceptable methods of worship must be based on the ways of worship found in the Bible; and

(2) acceptable worship should be directed to the triune God and to him alone.

Since all methods of worship must conform to these principles, every new method, by virtue of its newness, must be carefully analyzed to be sure that it does indeed conform. An example of an acceptable new method of worship employed by several churches is as follows:

- Conduct a complete worship service, with all of its traditional parts, in the Sunday morning hour.
- Conduct a very short service in the evening hour, with no sermon.
- In place of the evening service conduct a discussion of the pastor's morning sermon.
- All present can discuss together in one group moderated by the pastor, or several small groups can meet separately, moderated by elders.

Another example of an acceptable new method of worship would be

---

* Westminster Confession of Faith, Chapter 21.

to have the Sunday School just before the evening worship service, thus reserving Sunday morning solely for worship.

A word of warning is needed, however, to safeguard the mission church from the danger of using *experiments in worship* as if they were *new methods of worship*. "Experimental worship" is usually promoted by those who do not hold to conceptual truth and who feel that the purpose of the church is to reconcile man to man rather than to be an instrument by which the Holy Spirit reconciles man to God.** Because of these presuppositions the purpose of experimental worship seems to produce an experience (often traumatic) which lifts the participant to what appears to be new heights of insight into life. Experimental worship, as warned against here, pays no heed to the principles of acceptable worship. Rather, it makes the significance of the individual's experience of such magnitude that the goal becomes that of directing insight to the participant rather than directing worship to God.

One method of experimental worship is to create a situation conducive to "sharing yourself." As the bars of personal restraint are let down in this sharing, forces are developed out of the ensuing group interplay which challenge and often change one's attitudes about life. This experience is then called "worship." For instance, a church sanctuary might be arranged so that a dozen or more flags, banners or possibly advertising posters were located in different places, with a few chairs around each one. Each person attending the service would be invited to choose the banner which interested him (either for a positive or negative reason). He then would become part of a small group and each participant would be expected to share his personal reaction to the banner as he understood it in today's world. He would also be expected to react to the comments of others in the group, thus creating the possibility that this sharing of themselves would develop forces upon the group such that the attitudes of each participant would be challenged and possibly changed. This experience would be considered "worship."

** Dr. G. Aiken Taylor, in the April 1, 1970, issue of *The Presbyterian Journal*, attacks ". . . the current view that the church is the agent of social equalization, that the promise of social equalization is her message and that the practice of social equalization is her mission."

Obviously, "sharing yourself" is not in itself wrong, even as a part of worship. But, simply to have such interplay without regard for the principles of worship is wrong. Worship is directed to God, not to man.

Another method of experimental worship is to create a situation conducive to shocking the participant into a new insight into life. For instance, as each individual came into the sanctuary he might be given a face mask to wear for most of the service. The service would probably use a skit in order to dramatize a social ill currently under discussion. At the climactic point of the dramatization, everyone present would be told in a forceful way that every citizen must assume a responsibility actively to correct the social problem. Next, everyone present would be told that this responsibility starts with himself. Therefore each participant is under obligation. Then, each one present would unmask, see just who were sitting around him, and be asked to contemplate two issues:

(a) What do these people think of me in the light of this obligation?

(b) What about these people in their own lives?

This experience could well produce a shock that in turn would challenge and possibly change one's attitude toward life. This experience would be considered "worship."

Obviously, it is not wrong to experience a shock, even in a worship service, and thereby be persuaded to change one's attitudes and activities. But a shock for shock's sake, without regard to the principles of worship, is wrong. Again, it must be pointed out that worship is directed to God, not to man.

Before going on to discuss the second factor of influence, one additional aspect of the matter of worship must be presented. The mission church must consider the biblical injunction to guard the truth presented in worship. The Apostle John put it this way: "Look to yourselves, that we lose not those things which we have wrought . . ." (II John 8). He goes on to instruct his readers that anyone who does not believe that Jesus was God in the flesh should not be permitted to lead the flock in worship. (". . . receive him not into your house [church], neither bid him God-speed: For he that biddeth him God-speed is partaker of his evil deeds.") Therefore this need to guard the truth presented in worship must be considered when the declaration of purpose is framed.

(2) *Personal Lives.* Paul states the goals for our personal lives many times. For instance, ". . . denying ungodliness and worldly lusts, we should live soberly, righteously, and godly, in this present world" (Titus 2:12). "I beseech you therefore, brethren, by the mercies of God, that ye present your bodies a living sacrifice, holy, acceptable unto God, which is your reasonable service. And be not conformed to this world: but be ye transformed by the renewing of your mind, that ye may prove what is that good, and acceptable, and perfect, will of God" (Romans 12:1,2). The purpose to be accomplished by the impression made by us as individuals is explicitly declared by our Lord in the Sermon on the Mount: "Let your light so shine before men, that they may see your good works, and glorify your Father which is in heaven" (Matthew 5:16).

However, as this subject is analyzed, a potential danger must be recognized. The usual result of a discussion of this factor of influence is the cataloguing of a list, which in turn becomes a legalistic code. Such a list usually carries with it the unwritten presumption that those who conform are "in" and those who do not are "out." The solution to this may well be that a list, *per se,* not be constructed but that great stress be laid on the need to challenge the conscience of each friend and member and unreservedly to respect the right of each one to have his own conscience before God.

Further, it should be remembered in the course of discussion that a healthy church is one whose members are constantly experiencing spiritual growth and demonstrating more and more of the fruits of the Spirit. The healthy church will have:

- the unsaved coming as onlookers, some of whom will be saved and become babes in Christ;
- babes in Christ, who must be loved, protected and fed, most of whom are growing into spiritually mature children of God, yet are developing at differing rates and hence are scattered over the whole spectrum of spiritual growth;
- mature children of God who in turn assume more and more responsibility to proclaim the Word of God, so that,

• still more unsaved are coming as onlookers.

Finally, the analysis of the personal lives of the members as a factor of influence must also include the necessity that the Christian, even while growing in grace, likewise be steadfast for the faith against unbelief. (Jude 3: ". . . and I exhort you that ye should earnestly contend for the faith which was once delivered unto the saints.")

(3) *Programs.* Chapter fifteen will discuss ideas for outreach, which are essentially programs for the mission church to use. One area not covered in that discussion is the relationship between the mission church and the civil activities of the neighborhood, such as public holidays, municipal government appeals to the churches, citizens' committees of the public schools, etc. The precise responsibility the church should accept with regard to these matters of civil activities will vary from circumstance to circumstance, but should not be ignored, as is so often done by churches in the evangelical camp. Each church must reflect the description given us by our Lord himself, that we are "in" the world, even though we are not "of" the world (John 17:16, 18). The church must be prepared mentally as well as physically to be a tool of God in its neighborhood for righteousness and for actions for worthy progress in which it may be called for participation.

As far as the general program of the church is concerned, stress must be placed on the use of many people of the church, not just the "preacher." Too often the pastor and a few people do most of the work, and because there is an evidence of movement and activity it is hard for the pastor to comprehend that a serious sapping of the intrinsic strength of the church is actually taking place. Paul's admonition to the church at Ephesus shows that a healthy church uses the people: "And these were his gifts: some to be apostles, some prophets, some evangelists, some pastors and teachers, to *equip* God's people *for work in his service,* to the building up of the body of Christ" (Ephesians 4:11,12, NEB).

(4) *Buildings.* At this point in the life of the mission church a building is seldom on the immediate horizon. The purchase of land, however, is usually very much in the picture. In order both to help guide the decision as to the land to be selected and to complete the concepts being hammered out for the initial declaration of purpose, several

principal considerations must be worked out concerning the building even at this early stage.

a. *The location*

- must be accessible and have a high degree of visibility,
- and must be large enough to accommodate the ultimate plant (to include a Christian day school?) plus sufficient area for parking to conform to local ordinances for off-street parking.

Therefore a basic statement must be drafted to be incorporated into the initial declaration of purpose relating the location and size of property to the specific purpose of the church.

b. *The building(s),* no matter the cost, must primarily reflect the purpose of the church regarding its relationship to the community. Only secondary consideration should be granted to the personal preferences of individuals within the church. Therefore a basic statement must be drafted to be incorporated into the initial declaration of purpose relating the architecture of the building(s) to the specific purpose of the church.

(5) *The ultimate size* to which it is anticipated the church will grow must be tentatively fixed as a major factor contributing to the initial declaration of purpose. The decision will be the premise upon which architectural plans will be laid, to be sure. However, even though the building construction may be in the distant future, the decision about ultimate size will be significant from the beginning. For instance, it is necessary to determine whether the candidates for the pastorate believe they are called to minister to a church of that size.

Several practical guidelines should be brought into focus in drafting a statement relating size to the specific purpose in the initial declaration of purpose:

An exact maximum number of members should not be set. Rather, the declaration should indicate the minimum number of members (i.e., the lowest number necessary to accomplish the specific purpose of the church) and the maximum number of members (i.e., the greatest number with which the specific purpose of the church can still be accomplished).

The following procedure may help to set the minimum and maximum figures. However, care must be taken to evaluate its answers in the light of the other practical guidelines listed in this material:

- Determine what type of ministry the pastor will be expected to have, based on the specific purpose already adopted.
- Next, seek the advice of experienced men as to the approximate number of people a qualified pastor can serve in the light of this type of ministry.
- Next, make an educated guess of minimum and maximum numbers based on these considerations.
- Next, survey the incomes of the community the church anticipates serving, determine an average figure and then make a conservative estimate of projected church income at the minimum and maximum levels; determine whether or not a total and vital church program can be maintained at these levels (e.g., a church program which does not fail to challenge the members in their stewardship, yet does not expose the members to experience after experience of being forced to substitute presumption for faith).
- Finally, establish minimum and maximum figures which reflect the results of this study.

Also, it must be remembered that there are differing advantages in the small church and in the large church. The most apparent advantage of the small church is that it is easier to maintain an atmosphere in which each individual senses that he is needed and that he belongs. The most apparent advantages of the large church are that one outstanding pastor can minister to more people at the same time, and that the church can assist more when new opportunities or emergencies arise.

Again, the possibilities of having, in due time, an assistant pastor and of conducting several Sunday morning services should be considered as potentials within the framework of the specific purpose of the church.

14
The Mission Church:
Its Constitution and Bylaws

I. KEY SCRIPTURAL PRINCIPLES ON WHICH THE CONSTITUTION AND BYLAWS ARE BASED

Preliminary Notes:

1. It should be emphasized that this section is not designed to be an exhaustive examination of the doctrines of the church and of church government. However, a survey of the biblical basis for the major concepts of these doctrines is provided as the foundation upon which to construct the constitution and bylaws.

2. Although historical reference will be made to the church as it existed in the Old Testament dispensation, the fundamental concepts of the church in the New Testament dispensation are those specifically relevant to our day, and will be the ones used throughout this discussion.

3. The necessity of the church today was discussed in chapter one and will therefore be assumed throughout this discussion.

4. Several kinds of church government will be discussed. It is the author's conviction that God has seen fit to use and to bless the use of each kind of church government at one time or another. Again, it is his conviction that no particular kind is ever any better than the spiritual caliber of the men in the offices of the church.

5. A chronological survey of the church shows that it has always been

governed, but in a variety of ways! An extremely abbreviated survey is as follows:

Adam until Samuel:	*THEOCRACY*
Samuel until captivity:	*MONARCHY*
Apostolic history:	*APOSTOLIC-REPUBLIC*
Post-Apostolic until today:	*HIERARCHY and/or DEMOCRACY and/or REPUBLIC*

6. The *hierarchical* form of church government took over directly after the time of the apostles and was virtually the only type of church government until the Protestant Reformation. It is often called a bishopric. The Roman and Anglican churches are among quite a few practicing it today. The primary source of its strength lies in the fact that only the bishop can lay the hands of ordination on anyone.

The *democratic* form of church government is widespread today. It basically uses the vote of the majority of the members to make decisions. It has, in some instances, been developed as a check and countercheck system between the people and the pulpit. The Baptist and Congregational churches are among those practicing this kind of church government today.

The *republican* form of church government is based on representative government. From among the members of the congregation men who are quite evidently blessed with leadership ability and who are spiritually qualified are elected and given responsibility to carry out *designated* tasks. The people maintain their ultimate responsibility by determining who is elected to office and how long he then stays in office. Presbyterian churches use this form of church government.

A. *The controlling authority for church government*

The three kinds of church government are simply ways in which finite men exercise responsibility for the maintenance and extension of the church. Regardless of the form of government chosen, evangelical churches normally incorporate into their finished constitutions statements and provisions which demonstrate:

- that God created man as both a spiritual and material being, and that both natures of man must be dealt with in the development of the individual members of the church;

* that God himself—the Holy Spirit—performs this ministry on the basis of principles which are revealed in the Bible.

Fundamental to the exercise of church government is the fact that Jesus Christ is the head of the church. This may only be evident as the deduction from the logic involved in the documents of the church's government, or it may be explicit in the documents. In either case, the statements and provisions become meaningless aside from this fundamental. Therefore, regardless of the kind of church government adopted, the ultimate, controlling authority behind the government is not a man or a group of men; it is Jesus Christ himself, the head of the church!

Paul does not hesitate to state this fact: "And he is the head of the body, the church: who is the beginning, the firstborn from the dead; that in all things he might have the pre-eminence" (Colossians 1:18). "Let no man beguile you of your reward in a voluntary humility and worshipping of angels, intruding into those things which he hath not seen, vainly puffed up by his fleshly mind, and not holding the Head, from which all the body by joints and bands having nourishment ministered, and knit together, increaseth with the increase of God" (Colossians 2:18-19).

Stating the same truth in other terms, Paul tells Timothy that Jesus Christ is his King. Paul points out that Jesus has always been the King and that he will always continue to be the King (Paul refers to Jesus as "the King eternal") and hence admonishes Timothy to recognize him and worship him as the King right here and now: "Now unto the King eternal, immortal, invisible, the only wise God, be honour and glory for ever and ever. Amen" (I Timothy 1:17). It is not by accident, by the way, that many of the Scottish Reformers and the Puritan fathers referred to Jesus as "King Jesus."

A word must be given here for those mission churches which are related to denominations. The only way in which Jesus Christ will actually be maintained as head of the entire denomination is to be certain that each local congregation of the denomination unashamedly maintains him as head of their local congregation, come what may!

B. *The church as a body of believers, each of whom is individually important*

Today the word "church" usually evokes the idea of "institution," at best "religious institution." This term in turn implies an impersonal organization, dedicated to profit making or possibly to some vague altruism, but which has little or no desire to deal with the experiences and longings of the individuals involved with it.

This concept degrades the church members into an impersonal mass of humanity, the individuals of which have in effect become members without identity. This is contrary to the Bible.

The church is a body of believers, each of whom is important as an individual. In the true church, the members can never be treated as an impersonal mass of humanity. This is such a major factor in the development and maintenance of the church that it is insufficient to simply state the principle: it must be supported from the Bible.

A study of God's saving grace shows that God deals with each person he saves as an individual. The logical conclusion can be drawn that his church, the body of believers, must also maintain the individuality of the believer.

Jesus himself has declared that salvation is personal, that it is actually the reconciliation of an individual with God: ". . . and he calleth his own sheep by name, and leadeth them out. . . . I am the good shepherd: the good shepherd giveth his life for the sheep. . . . I am the good shepherd, and know my sheep, and am known of mine" (John 10:3b, 11, 14). "In the last day, that great day of the feast, Jesus stood and cried, saying, If any man thirst, let him come unto me, and drink. He that believeth on me, as the scripture hath said, out of his belly shall flow rivers of living water" (John 7:37-38). Paul called God "the justifier of him which believeth in Jesus" (Romans 3:26).

God not only deals with each as an individual in his salvation, but also does so in his continuing provision for his needs and his growth in Christ. For instance, God invites the Christian to pray to him directly and confidently because he knows each Christian as an individual and helps him personally. ". . . for your Father knoweth what things ye have need of, before ye ask him" (Matthew 6:8b). "Let us therefore come boldly unto the throne of grace, that we may obtain mercy, and find grace to help in time of need" (Hebrews 4:16). "And we know that all things work together for good to them that love God, to them who are the called according to his purpose" (Romans 8:28).

Finally, God's promises for the future are for us as individuals. Note the emphasis on the singular pronoun in these promises: "He that hath an ear, let him hear what the Spirit saith unto the churches; To him that overcometh will I give to eat of the tree of life, which is in the midst of the paradise of God" (Revelation 2:7). "Blessed and holy is he that hath part in the first resurrection: on such the second death hath no power, but they shall be priests of God and of Christ, and shall reign with him a thousand years" (Revelation 20:6). "Beloved, now are we the sons of God, and it doth not yet appear what we shall be: but we know that, when he shall appear, we shall be like him; for we shall see him as he is. And every man that hath this hope in him purifieth himself, even as he is pure" (I John 3:2-3).

These Scripture texts evidence that God's saving grace is given to each recipient as an individual, not as an impersonal part of a massive whole. Therefore, the logical conclusion is that the membership in the true church can never be treated as an impersonal mass of humanity.

Furthermore, the Bible specifically declares that the individuality of each church member must be respected.

In dealing with the problem of pride arising from special gifts of the Spirit, Paul lays great stress on the value of each person as an individual precious to the Lord. This is evident from the entire twelfth chapter of I Corinthians, a few verses of which will serve to demonstrate the truth: "For as the body is one, and hath many members, and all the members of that one body, being many, are one body: so also is Christ" (verse 12). "For the body is not one member but many" (verse 14). "But now hath God set the members every one of them in the body, as it hath pleased him. And if they were all one member, where were the body?" (verses 18-19). "For our comely parts have no need: but God hath tempered the body together, having given more abundant honour to that part which lacked: That there should be no schism in the body; but that the members should have the same care one for another. And whether one member suffer, all the members suffer with it; or one member be honored, all the members rejoice with it. Now ye are the body of Christ, and members in particular" (verses 24-27). The documents of the church's government, therefore, must specifically reflect this principle. They dare not take it for granted.

C. Qualified men as church officers

No matter which basic form of church government is used by a congregation, local men must assume the responsibility of church officers. Some churches delegate much responsibility to these men, while others delegate little responsibility. The individual church will determine the particular option to be adopted.

In the Bible the term "elder" is used for those to whom God has given the responsibility of spiritual oversight. It is helpful to distinguish between "ruling elders" and "teaching elders." Both the laymen and the minister serve as ruling elders. Because the minister's primary task, however, is to teach the truth of God to his people, he is called the teaching elder. ("Let the elders that rule well be counted worthy of double honour, especially they who labour in the word and doctrine" I Timothy 5:17.) But whatever title is used in a church today,* the Bible makes it abundantly clear that laymen do have major responsibilities for the spiritual condition of the church members. As to biblical evidence of this, Paul instructs the elders of the churches of Ephesus to: "Take heed therefore unto yourselves, and to all the flock, over the which the Holy Ghost hath made you overseers, to feed the church of God, which he hath purchased with his own blood" (Acts 20:28). The writer to the Hebrews admonishes: "Obey them that have the rule over you, and submit yourselves: for they watch for your souls, as they that must give account, that they may do it with joy, and not with grief: for that is unprofitable for you" (Hebrews 13:17).

Therefore, although some elders only rule in the church while others rule with them but also labor in expositing the Bible, the ruling elder is fundamental to the church.

The term "deacon" is used for those who primarily serve the physical

---

* As indicated in the "Definitions," the title "elder" is being used throughout this book for laymen who are called on to take responsibilities over spiritual matters in a church.

needs of others, such as Philip and Stephen, who served tables to relieve the apostles of the task (Acts 6:5). The office of deacon is also of great spiritual significance to the church. The term itself is a glorious title, referring to ministration in the work of God. Paul uses it for himself in Ephesians 3:7: "Wherefore I was made a minister [literally translated "deacon"]."

D. Qualifications for elders and deacons

I Tim. 3:1-13 and Titus 1:6-9 are the prime Scripture texts that specify the qualifications of these men. It is of importance that Paul declares that they be not "novices" (neophutos—newly planted). His implication is clear: their lives must have been consistently pure for a sufficient time that the church knows them by deed as well as word.

E. Method of choosing qualified officers

These men are normally inducted into office by submitting to the vow of ordination. This implies election by the people. (The word cheirotoneo—to appoint by vote—is the word translated "ordain" in Acts 14:23: "And when they had ordained them elders in every church, and had prayed with fasting, they commended them to the Lord, on whom they believed.") By this method the people selected and then the apostles set apart Stephen and the others, as recorded in Acts 6:5-6: "... and they chose Stephen ... and Philip ... whom they set before the apostles and when they had prayed they laid their hands on them."

F. The church must be duly subject to civil laws

Although the Bible makes it abundantly clear that the Christian must have his conscience in ultimate subjection to only one King, Jesus, the Bible also makes it just as clear that the Christian, and therefore the body of believers, must be in subjection to state authority if there is no usurpation of Christ's commands by the state. In the letter to the Romans Paul speaks out clearly: "Let every soul be subject unto the higher powers. For there is no power but of God: the powers that be are ordained of God" (13:1). "For he is the minister of God to thee for good. But if thou do that which is evil, be afraid; for he beareth not the sword in vain: for he is the minister of God, a revenger to execute wrath upon him that doeth evil. Wherefore ye must needs be subject, not only for wrath, but also for conscience sake" (13:4-5). "Render therefore to all their dues: tribute to whom tribute is due; custom to whom custom; fear to whom fear; honour to whom honour" (13:7).

On this premise, the church must respect the laws of the state as to finances, taxes, etc. The church must be prepared to live in the scriptural position before the state if it is to be truly in the scriptural position before God.

II. THE CONSTITUTION AND BYLAWS (AND THE CHARTER)

A. *Definitions*

The constitution of the church is primarily a document of principles which are the foundation upon which the church life and its operation are structured and which are not expected to change.

The set of bylaws is primarily a document of implementation of the principles enunciated in the constitution. Therefore, it must be flexible, reflecting the changes occurring in the church from its growth and increased outreach.

For purposes of incorporation it is best to use the charter, if it is at all possible according to state law, because it is the least complicated document possible and can be drafted in a very short time. If this is done, the work of drafting the constitution and bylaws can be delayed until four months after the mission church has begun to meet, thus affording the necessary time to assure that they will reflect more mature judgment about the individuality of the church.

B. *Guidelines for using the material on the constitution and bylaws*

For the sake of ease in using this material, an outline form of a constitution and of a set of bylaws is provided. Several guidelines should be kept in mind in the use of this material:

a. This is not the only possible order.

b. Some states may demand more or less in the documents.

c. Professional legal counsel *should* be sought to assist in the drafting of the material, but it *must* be used to review the completed documents before their final adoption.

A note of explanation is needed as to the potential use of this material. Each article and each section has at least one statement of description accompanying it. In several places, particularly in the bylaws, the descriptive material is quite lengthy. It is intended to be a source of reference for the principles involved in the material under discussion. As such, it is very probable that it is too detailed for the actual documents themselves.

C. *Contents of the Constitution:*

ARTICLE I
NAME

Name of the church. If the church is part of a denomination, the relationship should be indicated.

ARTICLE II
PURPOSE

This statement is of far greater importance than most groups realize. The purpose for the very existence of the church today is being challenged far and wide. A definitive statement, related directly to the Bible, is needed. It need not be long, but must be explicit. To this statement will be added the declaration of specific purpose when it is adopted in its final form.

ARTICLE III
DOCTRINAL STATEMENT

For those mission churches connected with a denomination, the doctrinal standards of the denomination are probably clearly stated in one form or another, so that reference to them is sufficient at this point. However, if they are not clear enough or do not have sufficient detail to satisfy the mission church, the necessary clarifications and/or additions should be made.

For those mission churches not connected with a denomination, a careful study of the statements of sister churches will prove a prime source of guidance in constructing this statement.

Every statement must be framed to accomplish the following goals:

1. Major doctrinal standards must be distinguished from minor, local practices or statements of pious advice in order to avoid constructing a statement that will either keep potential members from joining because it is more authoritative than the Bible or inject the possibility of heresy trials on matters which are basically of a subjective nature.

2. Each portion of the statement must be explicit and easily comprehended.

3. Each concept of the statement must be based on Scripture and the pertinent Scripture texts should be stated.

4. The overall statement must not be too long.

5. The overall statement must be an expression which will be adaptable to general use in the development and extension of the church as both the groundwork for and the boundary to this development and extension.

ARTICLE IV
GOVERNMENT OF THE CHURCH

For those mission churches connected with a denomination, the governmental standards of the denomination are probably clearly stated, so that reference to them is sufficient at this point. If they are not clear enough or do not have sufficient detail to satisfy the mission church, the necessary clarifications and/or additions should be made.

For those mission churches not connected with a denomination, a careful study of the statements of sister churches will prove a prime source of guidance in constructing this statement.

For every mission church, careful consideration should be made of the principle of dividing the work of the congregation and the corporation. The technical difference usually is that the corporation is made up of all the members of the congregation who are 21 or older. The practical difference is that the congregation deals with matters spiritual and the corporation deals with matters temporal. This division is not mandatory, but in principle and in practice it is advantageous and therefore it will be followed throughout this discussion.

Every statement must be framed to accomplish the following goals:

1. These statements must be limited to declarations of major policy. The details of application are worked out in the bylaws.
2. Each portion of the statement must be explicit and easily comprehended.
3. The overall statement must not be too long.
4. The overall statement must be an expression which will be adaptable to general use in the development and extension of the church as both the groundwork for and boundary to this development and extension.

ARTICLE V
MEMBERSHIP

Most churches have two or, at the most, three kinds of membership.

a. Communicant members of a particular church are persons who have made a credible profession of faith in our Lord Jesus Christ, who are believed to have been regenerated, whose Christian profession is not contradicted by flagrant sin or false doctrine, who are willing to submit themselves to the government of the particular church (and the denomination), and who have presented themselves to the elders of the particular church.

b. For churches holding to pedobaptism, an additional kind of membership is the non-communicant member. Non-communicant members of the church are children of communicant members or children under the care of communicant members who stand to them as foster parents in the place of parents. One or both parents or foster parents of these children shall be under solemn obligation to bring them up "in the nurture and admonition of the Lord."

c. Many churches, especially if they are located near a college campus, also maintain an associate membership: those believers temporarily residing at too great a distance from their permanent homes to worship and serve regularly in the churches of which they are members. Such believers, without ceasing to be communicant members of their home churches, may be received as associate members, and as such may enjoy all the privileges of fellowship, worship and service under the care of the pastor and spiritual officers of the church of which they become associate members, except that they may not vote in congregational and corporational meetings, and may not hold office for the congregation or corporation. The home church of the associate members will be notified of their reception as associate members and the home church will receive notice of baptism, weddings and funerals involving associate members and their families, and of any need for the administration of judicial discipline.

It is strongly urged that no "inactive roll" be maintained. If the member ought to be deprived of his vote, then some form of discipline should be exerted in order to win him back to full participation. If this is not successful, he should be taken from the roll. To place him on an "inactive roll" is usually a means of condemning him without trial or, at best, relegating him to a second-class citizenship in the church. In the case of those who have moved far away, special consideration should be made without resorting to this approach.

ARTICLE VI
OFFICERS

Some churches do not put any statement concerning officers into the constitution, but reserve the entire subject for the bylaws. If the constitution must be used as a charter, or if the mission church chooses to state the principle involved at this point, it is sufficient to name the various kinds of officers and give only a summary statement of job description.

- Elders, as technically used in this book: those charged with the spiritual welfare of the church.
- Deacons: those charged with assisting any who are in physical need.
- Trustees: those empowered to carry out the directions of the corporation concerning the financial and real estate business of the corporation.

It is strongly urged that the mission church make the elders also the trustees, so that the proper balance of spiritual oversight with financial decisions is maintained. Much of the mechanical work of the trustees can of course be delegated to others, as long as the trustees maintain the full sense of responsibility.

ARTICLE VII
AMENDMENTS

The procedure to amend the constitution must be workable but difficult, whereas amending the bylaws ought to be considerably easier. Some mission churches choose to make the article on doctrine unamendable.

A suggested formula is:

This constitution can be amended:

a. by a ¾ vote

b. at each of two duly called consecutive meetings of the congregation, which are not less than two weeks apart

c. only after the proposed amendment has been announced from the pulpit for two consecutive weeks previous to the first congregational meeting, and

d. only if each member has received, at least five days before the first congregational meeting, a letter stating the proposed amendment.

D. *Complications of changing the constitution*

If the constitution is also serving as a charter, any change in it must be recorded with the office of the Secretary of State in order to make it legally binding.

E. *Contents of the bylaws*

ARTICLE I
THE CONGREGATION

Section 1, Membership:

Limited to the standards given in Article V of the Constitution

Section 2, Responsibilities:
Include:
a. call of the pastor;
b. election of elders, deacons;
c. regular review and evaluation of the total ministry of the church;
d. if a denominational church, review of the total ministry of the denomination;
e. other ecclesiastical matters of concern.

Section 3, Mechanics of Operation:
Include:
a. naming the moderator for meetings.
b. time for regular stated meetings. Note: in setting these dates, give sufficient time for the completion and circulation of reports between the close of the church's fiscal year and the date of the meeting.
c. mechanics of calling regular stated meetings and special meetings. Note: care should be taken to be sure ample notice, both orally and in writing, is given to everyone. Also, means must be provided for the congregation to force a meeting if enough people are convinced one should be called.
d. Quorum. A suggested formula for determining the quorum is as follows:

- The quorum shall be a high percentage of the membership if the church is small.
- The percentage will decrease on a pre-set scale, in reverse proportion to the size of the congregation as it grows.
- The quorum will never be less than one-third of the membership.

It is urged that no *proxy* voting be allowed at all. The logic behind this recommendation is that the church recognizes that the Holy Spirit enables each member, because of his personality, his individual background and training, and his present walk in life, to see issues on an individual basis, and that the congregation needs the "cross-fertilization" of these points of view in order to be prepared to make intelligent corporate decisions.

e. Order. A statement such as the following is suggested: In conduct of meetings any parliamentary question not covered by this constitution and bylaws shall be decided by the latest edition of Robert's *Rules of Order.*

ARTICLE II
THE PASTOR

Section 1, Definition:

A statement such as the following is proposed: The pastor of this church shall be one who is duly ordained, called by the congregation of this church, and installed by due process.

Section 2, Qualifications:

A statement which includes references such as I Timothy 3:1-7, Titus 1:5-9 and I Timothy 5:17-18 is suggested. If there are any special denominational requirements, they should be stated at this point.

Section 3, Office:

A well-worded statement is necessary. All too often churches take the job description of the pastor for granted and later find they have no definitive position from which to make evaluations. The following is a model: "The office of pastor is first in the church, both for dignity and usefulness. He has different names expressive of his various duties; as the overseer of the flock he is Bishop; as he feeds them spiritual food he is Pastor; as he serves Christ he is Minister; as an example and as administrator he is Elder; as he bears the message of God he is Ambassador; as he dispenses the grace of God and administers the sacraments he is Steward. The Pastor shall be *ex-officio* a member of all committees of the church's lay officers."* In addition to this, some churches choose also to state that: ". . . although laymen may do many of the services described . . . yet the functions of a pastor, the administration of the sacraments of baptism and the Lord's supper, and

---

* *Form of Government of the Reformed Presbyterian Church, Evangelical Synod,* chapter 5, paragraph 4 b.

the blessing of the people by the divine benediction are reserved for the ordained and licensed minister."*

ARTICLE III
CALLING THE PASTOR

Introductory note: In all churches except those using hierarchical form of government the congregation calls the pastor. In many denominations, sources for candidates and the necessary chronological procedures have been predetermined for the local church. The material given below will be of most help to those churches not using the hierarchical form of government and to those not subject to a great many procedures whose chronology has been predetermined by a denomination. However, it is designed to be of help even to such churches.

Section 1, Preparation:
Certain fundamental principles must be woven into the material of this section.

a. The ultimate decision must realistically reflect the desire of a substantial cross-section of the people of the congregation.

b. The mechanics of preparation as set forth in the bylaws should be publicly reviewed, and the necessary committees established, *before* contacting any possible candidate.

c. In order to assure that the congregation's desire is realistically reflected, it should be determined whether special regulations are to be used for congregational meetings called for the purpose of issuing a call to a candidate. For example:

1. A minimum percentage of the family units of the congregation must be represented in order for the meeting to be considered legal. Notes: *a.* This quorum would be more restrictive than the usual quorum, which is based merely on a percentage of members; *b.* a family unit could be defined as that individual or family which is independently responsible for its way of life and which normally is financially independent; *c.* a family unit

---

* Ibid., 5, 4, c

is considered represented when any voting member of the family is present.

2. A minimum percentage of the eligible voters at the meeting must vote in the affirmative on the first ballot or, at the very least, on the second ballot in order to issue a call.*

d. Consideration must be given to the financial terms to be offered a candidate. If the separation of congregation and corporation is maintained, this is the business of the corporation. It must be understood that the terms in force for the previous pastor will not automatically be those to be offered to a new pastor. Also, a minimum and maximum set of terms may be adopted so that the pulpit committee will have a degree of flexibility to deal with the individual situation of each candidate.

e. A budget, or at least some kind of financial formula, should be adopted for the expenses to be incurred by the pulpit committee.

Section 2, Pulpit Committee:

It is suggested that a meaningful cross-section of the congregation be represented on the pulpit committee. One possible formula is as follows:

a. Representatives from each body of elected officers of the congregation should be on the committee, plus a representative from the Sunday School teachers or staff, from at least one of the women's organizations of the church (or from the women of the congregation at large) and from the teenage young people's group of the church.

b. Each group should elect its own representatives to the pulpit committee.

c. The committee should be large enough to be representative but

---

* This is not to be confused with the practice of taking an additional ballot in order to issue a unanimous call to the candidate. The rationale for such a call is to indicate to the candidate that, regardless of personal preference, all the members are prepared to "get behind" the candidate and support him. The author does not believe this is a good practice. It does not convey sufficient data to the candidate upon which to make a meaningful decision. In order to get this information the candidate is forced to ask for it, which often causes a slight tension that must be overcome, all of which is unnecessary. Therefore, it might be wise to word this section so that this practice is avoided.

small enough to function efficiently. For example, a congregation of 30 members may want a committee no larger than 10% of the congregation; a congregation of 300 may want a committee no larger than 5% of the congregation.

d. The committee should reflect the spiritual leadership of the church. To do so, the following provision is recommended:
- determine the quota of representatives (usually only one) each group will supply to make up the committee:
- authorize the elders to supply one more representative than each other group (i.e., if the quota for each other group is one representative, the elders will supply two representatives; if the quota is two per group, the elders will supply three representatives).

e. The first meeting of the committee should be convened by an elder and the first order of business should be to elect officers.

Section 3, Selecting the Candidate

The source of manpower available will depend on the kind of church; denominational churches will normally find their candidates within their denomination.

a. First, construct a large list of possible candidates—possibly ten or twelve. Note: if this is a denominational church, special care must be taken to follow correct governmental procedure if anyone on this list is not a member of the denomination.

b. Prepare a statement describing the church as to its declaration of purpose, its size, its history, its growth potential, etc. The statement need not be long. It must be approved by the elders of the church. Submit the *same* statement to each one on the list and request each to give the committee the following information:
   1. the individual's degree of interest in being considered;
   2. a biographical and professional resume;
   3. a list of three or four references.

c. Contact the references submitted and request information as to:
   1. preaching ability
   2. pastoral ability
   3. administrative ability

d. Assess the responses and construct a priority list of at least three *potential* candidates.

e. Prepare a list of thought-provoking questions that will provide an opportunity for the pulpit committee to make a comparative assessment of each man, based on the kind of subjects listed below:
   1. whether the man comprehends the declaration of purpose of this church and is able to relate to it;
   2. whether the man can "think on his feet";
   3. whether the man has the degree of commitment needed for the particular task;
   4. his attitude regarding the role his wife and his family will play in the church.

   The potential candidate will be asked these questions before the pulpit committee (not before the congregation) and he must have no forewarning of the questions. The same list will be used for each potential candidate, in order that it will be an objective criterion for assessment by the pulpit committee.

f. The pulpit committee should either:
   1. invite the potential candidates to the church to preach and be interviewed, or
   2. go to the churches of the potential candidates to hear them preach and to interview them.

g. During the interview with the potential candidate, the proposed terms for the call should be discussed and reaction to them noted by the pulpit committee.

h. The pulpit committee should then arrange for one of the potential candidates to come as *the* candidate.

i. Arrangements should be made to have the congregation meet to consider a call to the candidate within three to seven days after his candidacy.

j. Every potential candidate previously contacted must be told of the developments.

Section 4, The Candidacy

a. The candidate should spend with the calling congregation a minimum of four consecutive days, including Sunday, and preferably eight consecutive days, including two Sundays.

b. A schedule should be constructed to expose the candidate publicly and privately to as many people in the church as possible, including the children and young people.

c. The candidate must have freedom to ask questions and request data, so that he will be able to make an intelligent decision if he is called.

Section 5, The Call

a. If the vote is affirmative it must be communicated to the candidate and he should agree to a time limit within which he will reply.

b. If the vote is negative, the candidate must be notified. Then the church should repeat the procedure, probably turning to one of the remaining potential candidates.

ARTICLE IV
REMOVING A PASTOR

Section 1, Safeguards

1. This material must be safeguarded by Paul's admonitions: "Let the elders that rule well be counted worthy of double honour, especially they who labour in the word and doctrine" (I Timothy 5:17). "Against an elder receive not an accusation, but before two or three witnesses" (I Timothy 5:19).

2. An additional safeguard is also in order, as taught by Jesus for dealing with all men and therefore most certainly true in dealing with a pastor: "Judge not, that ye be not judged. For with what judgment ye judge, ye shall be judged: and with what measure ye mete, it shall be measured to you again" (Matthew 7:1-2).

   In order to avoid malicious and provocative accusations, the accuser must realize that he stands to be judged with the same severity with which he judges, if the accusation proves to be false.

3. All voting must be on written, secret ballots.

4. Matthew 18:15-17 describes the preliminary steps that ought to be taken in most cases. Every effort must be made to "win" the brother—even if he is the pastor! Even in those cases that may not seem to fit the particulars of Matthew 18:15-17, personal counseling is always wise. The elders must be extremely careful

to keep the name of Christ and of his church from degradation. If the situation must be "taken to the church," the procedures are described below.

Advice and counsel should be sought from ministers and officers of sister churches before and during any process to remove the pastor.

Section 2, Steps of Procedure

If the church is related to a denomination, the steps are usually detailed for the church. For those churches not having the steps delineated for them, the following guidelines should be incorporated:

a. In the case of an admitted act of immorality, the elders should be empowered to act without congregational authority, if a resignation has not been received within a reasonable time.

b. In the case of admitted advocacy of heresy, the elders must prepare a well-documented brief to present to the congregation, but may be empowered to act without congregational authority, if a resignation has not been received within a reasonable time.

c. In the case of an accusation of immorality or heresy which is denied, a congregation using the democratic form of government will vote after conducting a trial. For churches using the republican form of government, a system of balance and counterbalance is suggested, which is accomplished by placing the preliminary responsibilities (for a hearing and a recommendation) upon the elders but reserving the final decision for a vote by the people upon the recommendation of the elders. Almost every church using the hierarchical type of church government will be connected with a denomination and will have the details of this situation delineated for them.

Mention has been made of a trial and a hearing. The trial must be conducted with proper guidelines for procedure, and is intended to render a final verdict. The hearing must be conducted on the same high standard, but is not expected to render a final verdict. If a pastor does not choose to resign after the congregation has received the recommendation from the hearing, he may request the congregation to conduct a trial.

Great care must be taken to ascertain that a few do not "ramrod" a decision in order to have a pastor removed. It is suggested that the mechanics for calling such a meeting be more demanding than for normal congregational meetings, e.g., that the quorum be set higher than for normal congregational meetings, and that at least two-thirds (or possibly three-quarters) of the votes cast on the first ballot be in favor of the dismissal of the pastor.

d. In circumstances having nothing to do with morality or heresy, many of the above suggestions should be adopted but at least two modifications should be included:

1. the pastor should be first advised as to the problem, and specific efforts should be made to remedy the situation before any further steps are taken; and

2. the vote for his dismissal must be at least three-quarters of those voting, on the first ballot taken. This presumes in-depth personal counseling has already been undertaken. Some mention of the necessity for this might be given here.

(See Appendix G for a sample of how one church developed this section of the bylaws.)

ARTICLE V
THE BOARD OF ELDERS*

Note: Other titles may be used in the document instead of the term "Board of Elders," for instance: "The Diaconate," "The Session," etc.

Section 1, Composition

It is suggested that this board be composed of the pastor and the elders.

Section 2, Qualifications

Reference should be made to the Scriptures, particularly I Timothy 3:1-7 and Titus 1:5-9. Also, any specific prerequisites of a denomination should be listed. It is urged that these prerequisites be limited

---

* Note: If there are additional boards, such as a board of deacons, additional articles will be needed to cover each type. The material will be very much the same.

to major considerations without references to minor ethical practices which may vary according to circumstances, among people themselves, and, from time to time, even among those of like mind at any given moment.

Section 3, Structure and Tenure

It is proposed that there be classes of officers, each for a three year term, with each class completing its term in successive years. It is further proposed that there be a system of rotating out of office after one or at the most two successive terms, or at least to provide for this system when enough manpower is on hand.

Section 4, Meetings

It is proposed that regular meetings be held once a month. Provision must be made for special meetings and for ways by which the calling for a meeting may be forced.

Section 5, Officers

It is suggested that the pastor moderate these meetings, and that a secretary (clerk) be elected by the board each year from among themselves.*

ARTICLE VI
ELECTING CHURCH OFFICERS

Notes:
1. This material is applicable to all officers of the congregation. It may also be used for electing the trustees, who are the officers of the corporation. A statement must be made designating just what officers are covered by this article.
2. The necessity for several months of training has been discussed in chapter eleven. After the first election, each succeeding election should be scheduled several months after the nomination, in order to allow time for the training of all nominees. This proposition is taken as the foundation for this section of the bylaws.

Section 1, Nominating Committee

The membership of the nominating committee could be chosen in much the same way as that of the pulpit committee. The committee ought not be too large, and might well be based on a formula proportionate to the size of the communicant roll.

Section 2, Qualifications of Nominees

At least two mechanical prerequisites are mandatory:

a. They must be communicant members of the church at the time of the nomination, and

b. they must consent to spending the necessary time properly to fulfill the duties of their office if elected. Occasionally additional prerequisites are imposed, such as minimum number of years as a communicant member of the church before being nominated, although this type prerequisite can be too restrictive in some circumstances.

The spiritual qualifications are discussed in chapter eleven. Some reference must be made here to these qualifications.

Section 3, Procedure of Nominations

The details of this will reflect very directly the declaration of purpose of the church: for instance, whether or not nominations will be permitted from the floor, whether they are to be prescreened by the elders, etc.

Section 4, Congregational Meeting for Nominations

The date for nominations must be early enough so that there will be time for the training sessions before the election of officers at the annual congregational meeting.

Section 5, Preparation of Nominees

A statement is needed indicating any possible exceptions among the nominees who are to take the training course; who will conduct the course; who will conduct an examination, etc.

Section 6, Congregational Meeting for Election

A statement is needed making these elections part of the docket of the annual congregational meeting. If there are special requirements for election, or if the church desires to bypass any requirements of the number of years of membership for special cases, they must be stipulated. Any extraordinary bypass will probably be a direct reflection of the declaration of purpose adopted by the church.

Section 7, Ordination and Installation

A statement is needed of the maximum time allowed after the annual congregational meeting for ordination and installation to be accomplished.

ARTICLE VII
THE CORPORATION

Section 1, Membership

This is usually a statement that the membership of the corporation is constituted of all the members of the congregation who are 21 and over.

Section 2, Responsibilities

Include the following:

a. Achieve official status of a religious non-profit corporation (trusteeship, in some states).

b. Determine the pastor's salary and benefits.

c. Make decisions regarding the purchase or sale of all properties.

d. Determine plans and costs of all new building programs.

e. Make decisions regarding all major changes in existing buildings.

f. Other matters dealing with the physical concerns which the congregation duly refers to the corporation.

Section 3, Mechanics of Operation

Some churches merge the business of the congregation and the corporation. If this is done, care must be taken that corporate business is presided over by the proper corporate officer, especially if the pastor is expected to preside over the congregation but not the corporation. Beyond this, all the data given under Article I, section 3 of the bylaws would be relevant to this section. The corporation must set the dates of its fiscal year. An annual meeting should be scheduled at the time of the annual congregational meeting.

ARTICLE VIII
THE TRUSTEES

Section 1, Composition

It is suggested that each man elected to the office of elder also be invested with the office of trustee. The purpose of this proposal is to keep spiritual and material responsibilities related, thus avoiding one potential area of internal strife among church officers. However, three additional alternatives are possible:

a. The combined officers, i.e., elders and deacons, may be merged to form a board of trustees;
b. only the deacons may be invested with the office of trustee; or
c. a separate body of men may be chosen.

Section 2, Qualifications

If men elected to office as elders and/or deacons are used as trustees, probably no further qualifications will be needed. If the trustees are to be an entirely separate group of men, they must be willing to accept the system of doctrine adopted by the church. They will not be ordained, since the office of trustee fulfills not a biblical but a cultural (economic and legal) requirement.

Section 3, Responsibilities

A statement is needed that the trustees are responsible to hold title to, maintain and supervise all properties of the church, but are empowered to act only by instruction from the corporation, issued at a duly-called corporation meeting.

Section 4, Structure and Tenure

The data in the bylaws for the elder and deacon are pertinent here.

Section 5, Meetings

If the trustees are the elders or deacons, the work will be done during their regular meetings. If the trustees are a separate body of men or a combined body of officers, a regular program of meetings should be established. Provision must be made for special meetings, and for ways of forcing a meeting to be held.

Section 6, Officers

It is suggested that the trustees elect a president, a vice president, a secretary and a treasurer annually from among themselves.

Section 7, Financial Secretary

If the corporation chooses to have a financial secretary, ultimate responsibility must clearly remain in the office of the treasurer. It is probable that election to the office of financial secretary will be made upon recommendation from the trustees at the annual corporation meeting.

ARTICLE IX
AMENDMENTS

The procedure to amend the bylaws should not be as difficult as that to be followed in order to amend the constitution. A suggested formula is:

a. a majority vote,

b. at any duly-called meeting of the congregation or corporation.

15
The Mission Church: Its Development

"How do we reach new people?" This question is almost always the first one asked by the nucleus of seed families as they make the decision to become a mission church. This question must of course be motivated by the commitment to grow in order to bring glory to God, not simply to grow in order to stay alive or to be more influential than other churches. The necessity for such wholesome motivation is demonstrated by two axioms of church life which are all too easily observable:

- The church that does not continually serve new people in addition to its original members will stagnate spiritually and eventually die, regardless of the sincerity and piety of the original members.
- Even when there are many new people coming, unless a good number of them have been saved through the ministry of this church and its pastor this church will stagnate spiritually and eventually die, regardless of the size, the activity, and the growth rate of the church.

This chapter includes several methods to reach new people. In many instances additional blessings to the members themselves will be an extra incentive to use them. Each has been used and found to be successful.

Local circumstances probably will necessitate modifications in these plans. No attempt is made in this chapter to go into complete detail about organizing them, since their use may vary a great deal from church to church. It is not intended that these methods are to be used simultaneously.

Most of the methods that are presented are basic to any church and must be used from the very beginning. They are not to be discontinued as the church grows. They can be modified over and over again to adjust to growth and development, but are absolutely fundamental to all other methods and ideas.

Again, personal evangelism must be emphasized as the basic and most important single activity for any evangelical church's outreach and growth. While referring to its significance, the purpose of this book is not to duplicate many existing manuals that explain this important ministry of the church.

A warning must be given regarding the standard practice of house-to-house visitation. The suggestions in this chapter are based on a conclusion with which many disagree but which the author has repeatedly seen to be true: it is useless to visit house-to-house in an established neighborhood in an attempt to get visitors to church. The one possible exception would be the massive visiting and presentation program (see method two, chapter six). However, without a great deal of manpower to assist, even this method is unsuccessful. The combined use of the following suggestions will open direct contacts in any neighborhood, whether established or new.

A. Particular responsibilities of the organizing pastor.
  1. The organizing pastor must capitalize immediately on every opportunity that arises. No follow-up of an opportunity can be postponed or scheduled "next week"; his schedule must be flexible enough to take advantage of each circumstance as it arises.
  2. The organizing pastor must begin to delegate responsibilities to the families immediately. A rule of thumb to prod him in this direction is: "Don't do it yourself if you can get others to do it."

     Some of the jobs to be delegated are the tasks of welcoming guests, registering them in a guest book, calling them about meetings, inviting them to homes, etc. This is especially true of the families on the prime prospect list (see "B" below).
  3. The organizing pastor must institute training and evaluation sessions with each one to whom responsibility has been designated.

This is to ensure that the work is being done properly and to encourage the worker to grow in the Lord through the labor.

4. The organizing pastor must institute team training on the field for members, especially in evangelism. It has been proven over and over that it is not sufficient to conduct a class in evangelism and urge the people to put it into practice. Dr. James Kennedy has developed a program in which the organizing pastor personally trains one member on the field. That member then trains another while the organizing pastor is training a fourth, thus providing a constant program of multiplying the efforts to reach the lost.*

5. The organizing pastor should be provided with a supply of a classic book dealing with Christian living, and he should give a copy to each family when they join the church. At a later date he should call on the family and discuss the book with them.

6. The organizing pastor should be provided with a library and he should seek to follow up questions and discussions by loaning a pertinent book to the person or persons involved. After several weeks he should arrange a visit with the people and review the book or its key sections to be sure it is understood.

B. Contact lists

1. *Prime prospect list:* This list is comprised of families with whom some definite, often personal, contact exists. They may or may not be Christians. There should always be a minimum of ten families on this list. The primary sources for this list are:

- friends or relatives of seed families (seed families should have granted permission to use their names for an introduction);
- visitors to the services and/or Bible classes;
- referrals from any visits by the organizing pastor, the church officers and members of the congregation;
- for denominational mission churches: referrals from mailing lists of mission boards and agencies of the denomination;
- inquiries from general mailing and advertising (see no. 3 below).

---

* Dr. Kennedy is the pastor of the Coral Ridge Presbyterian Church, Fort Lauderdale, Florida. He has personally granted permission for his program to be presented. His book, *Evangelism Explosion,* was published by Tyndale House Publishers in 1970.

The first and most basic use of the prime prospect list is to engage in churchwide prayer for those on the list. (Note carefully: The burden in prayer must include the families' spiritual and physical well-being and the use of the mission church by the Holy Spirit to be a spiritual blessing to them. It is wrong simply to pray that they become members of the church.)

Next, each member of the mission church should be prepared to capitalize on any contact with each family on the list whenever and wherever an opportunity arises.

Next, each family on the prime prospect list must personally be visited within ten days after the name is placed on the list. Normally, it is wise to assume that the family visited is not a Christian family. Therefore, care should be taken to present the person and work of Christ in a clear and gracious manner.

Next, the organizing pastor himself should probably visit, prepared to deal with whatever spiritual problems may arise. Needless to say, a friendly invitation to the church must be extended at each visit and some piece of literature should be given.

2. *General mailing list:* This list is comprised of all the families who have shown interest in the church. It will include:

- all the seed families;

- all the prime prospect list;

- anyone who has been interested within the past two or three years (unless, of course, the family has specifically requested to have its name removed from the list).

The basic use of the list is to guarantee that some piece of literature of the church gets into every home on the general mailing list at least four times a year. This could well be announcements of special meetings, summer Bible school, Bible classes, etc. Each mailing should include some word of witness to the glory of God. Experience indicates that, although many families may not respond to these mailings, yet they are very aware of the concern that is demonstrated by this continued contact, and, in a time of crisis, will call upon the church for help. Therefore, it is wise to keep this list as large as possible.

3. *General announcement lists:* These lists are comprised of names with which no previous contact has been made. The purpose of these lists is to alert as many people as possible to the existence and the specific purpose of the mission church in order to solicit inquiries. There is no limitation as to the size of these lists. New sources of names should constantly be sought.

Several sources for these lists are:

• Any general mailing list which can be made available to the mission church. For instance, the mailing list of a store owner in the congregation; a purchased mailing list of every Baptist, or every Presbyterian, or every Methodist in the area, or everyone who formerly subscribed to a national magazine, etc.
• Saturation bulk mailing of a specific geographical area (see method four, chapter six).
• Newspaper advertising.

Extreme care must be taken in preparing the material that will be mailed out (or printed in the newspaper as an advertisement), to make it clear that everything which is done is for the sole purpose of constructing a bridge of communication. If anyone wants to visit the church, he must act on his own initiative to do so.

C. *New neighbor visitation ("Block" visitation).*

1. Divide the entire area to be reached by the mission church into sections. Assign each section to one person, family or team.
2. Each section is to be constantly patrolled to note each new house started and each "For Sale" sign that goes up, and to watch the progress of each.
3. While the new family is moving in, a church member should visit with:
   a. a brochure from the church, which has the name, address and telephone number of the organizing pastor printed on it;
   b. a personal invitation to the church (admitting that it is a bad time to visit) and assurance that the pastor will be glad to help in case an emergency arises, coupled with a promise to return in a few days;
   c. possibly a cake or casserole.

4. In two to five days the pastor should call to offer his personal invitation to church, attempt to emphasize the highlights of the gospel, and leave a different piece of church literature. He must decide whether to call again, how soon, and whether to send an elder.
5. If any interest is shown, laymen should also visit within the first two weeks.

D. *Neighborhood Bible classes.*

(Note: These classes may have already been started. See method one, chapter six.)

Within the first two months, neighborhood Bible classes should be started.

1. Suggestions:
   a. Limit to one hour.
   b. Start promptly.
   c. End promptly.
   d. Do not emphasize refreshments.
   e. Study a book of the Bible, such as the gospel of John.
   f. Constantly emphasize that any question may be asked and that every effort will be made to give an answer.
   g. Invite parents to bring children; a means of caring for them must be devised.
2. Probably seek to establish several Bible classes per week. Since daytime classes will attract only women, at least one per week should be conducted in the evening.
3. Individual visits to the home should follow up questions and discussions which arise during the classes.

E. *Children's classes and summer Bible school.*

Usually children's classes can be started very soon after the mission church is established. It should be pointed out that many people can effectively teach with a little help and training even though they originally feel that they may not be totally qualified.

The summer Bible school is a major part of the outreach of the mission church. Pupils should be enrolled in April for a June school. (This is about a month before other churches get to the families.)

Suggested program for a summer Bible school:

1. If at all possible, organize the school by grades rather than by departments.
2. Materials by Scripture Press and Gospel Light Press are good. Varieties of the material originally designed as the "Summer Bible School Program" by Dr. L. Latham, Chester, Pennsylvania, are excellent. Whichever material is used, the emphasis must be on the Bible, not on handcraft. It is suggested that handcraft be limited to the very youngest children only.
3. Enlist all teachers and helpers early in the spring. Conduct several training sessions as to methods and goals, and stress the need for coordinating the program, the schedule and the use of helpers.
4. Enlist the entire mission church to undergird the work with much prayer. The members will also be needed to help with car pools, enrollment of students and follow-up for absent students.
5. Do not take daily offerings for the expenses of the school. Possibly prepare the children to give their own sacrificial offering once a week to a mission project. In the closing exercises receive an offering from the parents to underwrite the expenses.
6. Stress the closing exercises; make them an excellent demonstration of the knowledge of the Bible and of the catechism which the children have gained; do not allow these exercises to be merely a meaningless jumble of pretty songs and poems unrelated to the work of the school.
7. Probably have a social after the closing exercises.
8. Within two months visit each new contact made through summer Bible school, dealing with any opening that presents itself and giving friendly invitations to the church.

F. *Children's and teenagers' activities.*

In some places the Christian Brigade movement or some similar type of group that instills Christian standards and discipline and provides opportunity for crafts and fun is very successful. The older teenagers do not usually respond to stereotyped programs, but do enjoy freer activities, such as young people's rallies and retreats, Christian coffee houses, etc. Every such activity must be under close supervision and each opportunity for spiritual growth capitalized on in the appropriate way.

G. *Couples' Club.*

Within the first five months a couples' club should be started. The degree of organization should purposely be kept minimal.

1. The purpose of the club is to deal with contemporary subjects from the Christian point of view. A secondary purpose is to afford an opportunity for fellowship.

2. The kind of topic appropriate is demonstrated by this list:

   • child discipline
   • Christian literature
   • the pill and birth control
   • the Christian parochial school
   • family devotions
   • teenage dating
   • conscientious objection to the draft
   • avoiding vs. evading taxes; deferred giving

3. Guest speakers, panels, discussion groups, etc. may be used. Some topics will demand specific answers, others will call for an airing of the various aspects of the question, leaving the decision up to the individual. The prerequisite upon which any program is based is that the Bible is the final authority for faith and practice.

4. The social aspect of this program ought to be a very real part of it, but probably emphasized only once every three or four months. (Note: The strength of a church is in its families, and a definite approach must be made to relate to entire families, starting with the husbands and wives. Other activities will have to be prepared for those who are single, or widows and widowers.)

H. *Emphasis on current religious news events.*

Consideration should be given to devoting the evening service once every other month to keep the congregation abreast of major developments in the religious field.

1. Material of international, national and local importance should be covered, with enough background given to make the presentation meaningful to the entire congregation.

2. In dealing with key issues, the principles involved should be developed and related to the Scriptures, the Scriptures exegeted, and,

if apropos, the people advised concerning the responsibility they
must bear as Christian citizens.

3. There should be no hesitation to deal with names and specifics, if
   it is always made abundantly clear that the question is one of facts
   and not one of the sincerity of those involved.
4. A format that has proven successful is as follows:
   a. An invocation.
   b. A "shot gun" presentation of developments at home and abroad
      in the religious world, with very little comment on each item
      beyond placing it in its context.
   c. A short break in the news presentation, by way of announce-
      ments, offering, etc., or
      A short break by a period of comments or questions on the ma-
      terial given thus far.
   d. An in-depth presentation of one or two religious news items
      with their relationship to Scripture. Occasionally an expert on
      the subject can be brought in for this material.
   e. A short period for comments or questions.
   f. An appropriate hymn of devotion.
   g. The benediction.

I. *Special meetings within three months.*

An intense weekend of special meetings (Friday night through Sunday
night) should be planned in order to:

- give the mission church encouragement;
- and enable the mission church to benefit from exposure to an
  emphasis needed at that particular point of its growth.

Usually an additional benefit is the opportunity to publicize these
meetings and make new contacts through them.

1. The meetings should normally follow a theme determined by the
   self-examination of the mission church and by the evaluation of
   the committee on assessment. The topic may be related to Christian living, some relevant subject under discussion on the local
   or national press, a particular aspect of Bible study, or any
   special need which the evaluation has uncovered. A "traditional" series of nightly evangelistic meetings would not normally be recommended.

2. The committee on assessment should help in planning these meetings and should propose ways and means to help underwrite their cost.

3. The speaker should be a man well qualified in his field.

Conclusion:

Again, it must be made very clear that these are only a few ideas. Each one has proven to be workable and of great value. The mission church must be ready to try new ideas when they are proposed. However, thorough prayer preparation and organizational responsibility are always needed before any program is put to work.

16
A Time for Decision:
Should a Particular Church Be Established?

This is the second major decision that must be made in establishing a church. The basis of both decisions must be conviction rather than mere circumstances. The committee on assessment must evaluate the progress in the light of the goals which have been set and then make a judgment as to whether or not the mission church is ready to become a particular church. In this situation, however, the organizing pastor and the members of the mission church must first have been convinced that God has indeed provided the development and that the mission church is *de facto* a particular church.

The objective evidence which convinces the committee on assessment of the mission church's growth and maturity is discussed in extended detail in chapters ten and eleven. The key facets of this evidence are:

(1) internal development, i.e., that the seed families have grown in grace and that specific tangible blessings have been experienced as to:
   - a vital prayer life;
   - a meaningful worship of God;
   - an ever-increasing application of doctrine in the personal lives of the members;
   - sincere Christian love for each other;
   - evidence of spiritually qualified elders, properly trained to assume the responsibility of spiritual oversight;

- drafting of a meaningful declaration of specific purpose and constitution and bylaws;
- evidence of meaningful progress, derived from regular evaluation and planning sessions; and

(2) external usefulness, i.e., that the mission church has been used as a blessing to additional families beyond the initial seed families.

PREPARATION FOR THE DECISION

The committee on assessment must review the goals which were adopted by the mission church when it was started, and any goals which have been set subsequently. These goals, be they specific data such as proposed financial budgets or the more intangible spiritual achievements such as increased comprehension and application of the church's system of doctrine, will serve the committee on assessment as measuring tools throughout its task of making a decision.

The committee on assessment must read all the minutes of the various meetings held throughout the mission church phase. This will enable it to determine whether the mission church has begun to use the spirit of its form of government in its attempts to set goals and to adopt the programs necessary to achieve those goals.

The committee on assessment must review all the documents which the mission church has produced (its declaration of specific purpose, its constitution and bylaws, etc.) to determine whether the mission church has incorporated the spirit of its system of doctrine and its form of government in its documents.

The committee on assessment must meet with the organizing pastor and hear his personal testimony as to the way in which God has worked in and through the mission church. It should be remembered that God, who is infinite, eternal and unchangeable, is working in this finite world and in finite men. Therefore the testimony should bear witness to more than statistics: it should bear witness to the power of the gospel at work. This testimony must give objective evidence of the growth and maturity already outlined above.

The committee on assessment must meet with all the men trained as potential elders to determine that God has indeed provided spiritually qualified, properly trained men to assume the responsibility of eldership. The committee on assessment must meet with the borrowed elders to determine their evaluation of the spiritual development and current situation of the mission church. The subjection of the members to the discipline of the church must be discussed, both as to administrative and judicial discipline. Some expression of the degree of willingness of the members to become subject to their own elders should be sought to determine whether or not God has provided the necessary maturity to make this transition. If any member of the mission church is under discipline of the borrowed elders, the situation should be reviewed and, if possible, an assessment made of the progress toward his restoration and of the attitude of the mission church toward the way in which the borrowed elders have handled the situation.

The committee on assessment must meet with the treasurer of the administrative committee to determine:

- that the bookkeeping is being properly done;
- that the mission church has met its financial obligations (or if not, why not);
- that the giving of the members of the mission church has evidenced their commitment;
- that the giving has been consistent (e.g., has not dropped off during the summer months) and has been increasing.

The committee on assessment must meet with some individual families in their homes and with the church as a congregation to determine something of the internal development and the external usefulness of the mission church.

MAKING THE DECISION

The committee on assessment must now wait on God for wisdom. It must be satisfied that:

- the church is composed of a body of believers who are both united and responsible; if the situation is such that the organizing pastor, or a few individuals, are controlling the group and the others are not taking their share of responsibility, the committee on assessment must decide either to continue the ministry as a mission church or to dissolve the mission church, rather than to overlook an anti-Biblical condition;

- the mission church has developed sufficiently that the whole counsel of God is being preached, the sacraments are correctly comprehended, appreciated and administered, and the members are willingly submissive to proper discipline for the sake of their own souls;
- the mission church has matured sufficiently that the objective evidence previously determined as the standard to be achieved has indeed been achieved;
- any physical or financial details which are unsettled are being properly handled.

If the committee on assessment is clearly not satisfied in any of the areas of judgment, it must either delay the beginning of phase three or dissolve the mission church.

If the decision is to keep the mission church as such for a while longer, the committee on assessment must explain its decision in such a way that it enables the mission church to benefit from the action. It should help the mission church to frame the necessary new goals for itself and a proposed time-table for their accomplishment.

If the evidence is that the mission church has not really been blessed by God, or to put it from man's point of view, it just has not worked out, the decision to dissolve no matter how difficult, must be made. The need to make such an objective decision has not often been understood, with the result that there are too many churches trying to have a meaningful ministry that are really not bringing glory to God. The conviction with which this whole formula was adopted in the first place, however, was that it was not sufficient just to have another church. Therefore, the responsibility of the committee on assessment to consider this action cannot be avoided.

If the committee on assessment is almost, but not quite, satisfied, it will be necessary to make a judgment as to what decision will produce the proper balance between incentive to go on and concern to do things decently and in order. If the decision is to delay, the committee on assessment should help the mission church to frame the necessary new goals for itself and a proposed timetable for their accomplishment. If, on the other hand, the decision is to proceed immediately to phase three, the committee on assessment should point out the weak spots, suggest ways to strengthen them and challenge the mission church to do all that is necessary to improve.

If, as is to be expected, the committee on assessment finds the mission church to be *de facto* a particular church, it will have an easy decision to make: simply concur with the pastor and the members of the mission church that phase two has been completed and that preparations should immediately be made to enter phase three by becoming a particular church.

PHASE III

17

The Particular Church:
Its Establishment

By this time, the mission church is *de facto* already a particular church! However, a definite set of actions are needed to make the transition official. They can be transacted one after the other, probably during an extended weekend.

Throughout the course of the transactions necessary to establish a particular church, several opportunities present themselves as natural circumstances for special messages in order both to re-emphasize the importance of the work involved and to give special praise and glory to God for his mercies and blessings. Each such circumstance should be used.

The committee on assessment should be responsible for making the arrangements and for transacting the business. The organizing pastor may well be used as the actual moderator for all the transactions except the calling of the pastor.

There are four areas which must be dealt with in the course of the transition from a mission church to a particular church.

1. *Membership.* Most mission churches will already have examined and received members to a communicant roll. At this time action must be taken to constitute this roll the charter roll of the particular church. This is done by a declaration to this effect by the committee on assessment after the work of the organizing pastor and the borrowed elders has been reviewed and found to be satisfactory. The

charter roll may be kept open for a period of time if the church so desires.

It is possible that the mission church phase was not long enough for receiving communicant members. Under these circumstances, the organizing pastor must have completed his training classes and be prepared to present candidates to the borrowed elders for examination. Those who give a creditable profession will be constituted the charter roll of the church.

2. *Constitution and bylaws.* By this time the mission church should have these finished and ready for adoption. The committee on assessment must study the draft. They may suggest refinements. The newly constituted congregation must then consider the suggested refinements and decide whether to accept them. It then must vote to adopt the documents. From this point on the congregation has committed itself to live under these documents. Therefore, even the remaining business of establishing itself as a particular church is to be transacted according to these documents.

3. *Election of elders and deacons.* The organizing pastor must have completed his in-depth training program for the eldership and the diaconate. The committee on assessment must now meet with all those trained and examine them. Those who are found to be qualified will then be presented to the newly constituted congregation as candidates for election to office. The congregation will then vote to elect its first official ruling body of men. The committee on assessment will then proceed to ordain and install those elected to their positions. (Each year thereafter, of course, the nominees will be determined according to the rules adopted in the bylaws.)

4. *Calling the first pastor.* It must be remembered that, up until this time, the mission church was in reality a non-self-governing body of believers who anticipated becoming a church. Before this time, therefore, it was not truly a particular church and therefore was not able to issue an official call.

In many instances, the organizing pastor will be called to become the first installed pastor of the particular church. Whether this is the case or not, the congregation must now, using its newly adopted bylaws, vote to extend a call to a minister of the gospel to become its pastor. Using the procedure of the denomination involved or the bylaws of the independent church, as the case may be, the pastor must be installed into this particular church. In the case of the independent church, the committee on assessment may well assume the responsibility for the installation so that this is done decently and in order.

Only after the first pastor is duly called and installed is the major work of the committee on assessment over. However, experience has shown that it is valuable to maintain a relationship, primarily one of consultation, for several years after the formal act of establishing the particular church.

Conclusion

All of these efforts have been directed toward preparing the group of believers to be a worthy particular church which is self-governing and self-sustaining, and has every reason to believe it will be able to continue as such until our Lord returns. The care and effort already expended must be maintained and, in some cases, even increased in order that the full potential of the future will be realized.

18

The Particular Church:
Its Building Program

Introduction

The building program should have three goals:
- to construct that particular building which best reflects the purpose of the church;
- to do so efficiently and at a reasonable cost;
- and to do so in a way which will further the spiritual growth of the people.

Too often a building program has only a building committee and a finance committee at work. At certain points in the program, when they are forced to get necessary legal sanction for finances, they return to the church corporation* for its stamp of approval. The committees actually proceed on their own and the corporation becomes the proverbial "rubber stamp." No building program is designed to produce the "rubber stamp" situation, to be sure, but most of them are conducted this way. The end result of this approach is often a lasting bitterness among the members of the church.

---

* The term "corporation" is used throughout this chapter, since the building program is basically the work of the corporation, not the congregation. This in no way is intended to imply that the work of the building program is business and therefore not to be a spiritual challenge to the congregation, with all its spiritual strength, with the exception that it is limited to those 21 and older.

In order for a building program to be both spiritually and physically effective, the corporation must maintain its position as the responsible agent, and should construct its building committee and finance committee as its servants.

However, the building program and all its committees must be dominated by a commitment to conceive of this program primarily as a spiritual pilgrimage so that the decisions of this unique experience in the church's life are safeguarded against purely pragmatic solutions. This attitude, therefore, must be both the motivation and the controlling influence for each of the developments of the program.

Before going into this program in depth, it seems wise to list several preliminary considerations and to make comment on them.

Corporation meetings.

Because of the pressures inherent in a building program, the corporation is often tempted to bypass the prerequisites for legally calling meetings. It is mandatory, however, that each meeting in which decisions are to be made be properly called and have at least a quorum. Also, when coming to the time of major decisions, it is often wise first to have the corporation meet as a quasi committee-of-the-whole several times in order to have ample opportunity to discuss the situation with no power to make motions and vote, before the corporation takes its vote.

Communication.

Care must be taken to keep the lines of communication open between the various committees and the corporation. In this regard, the building committee must be careful:

- not to work too far ahead in their plans without the members of the corporation having ample opportunity to express reactions and ideas;
- to have drawings and pictures on public display for each proposal, rather than to depend on verbal explanations; and
- to weigh the possibility of making a scale model of the building.

Composition of the building committee.

It should be a cross section of the church, yet must not be so large that it is impractical. A possible formula for its composition is:

- a representative of the elders, chosen by the elders;
- a representative of the deacons, chosen by the deacons;
- a representative of the Sunday School, chosen by the Sunday School;
- a representative of the young people, chosen by the young people;
- two or three representatives at large chosen by the corporation;
- with at least two or three of the members being women;
- the pastor as an *ex-officio* member.

The chairman of the committee should be qualified to act as a spokesman for the committee both to the corporation and to the professionals employed for the work.

Composition of the finance committee.

Normally this committee will be composed of the trustees of the church. But since this is not always the case, a separate committee called the finance committee is referred to throughout this chapter, in order to avoid confusion. If the finance committee is composed of the trustees, much duplication of work can be avoided.

Declaration of specific purpose.

It is mandatory that, at the outset, the principles expressed in the declaration of specific purpose be reviewed by the entire corporation and that the building committee be cognizant of them in detail. Also, these principles must constantly be used as a standard of comparison at each stage of development in order to assure the corporation that the end product will indeed be a tool to fulfill the specific purpose established for the church.

Role of the pastor.

From the point of view of the church, the pastor is its "professional." It is inherent in his office that he be knowledgeable about the proposed use of the building: its ability to fulfill both the specific purpose for the existence of this particular church in the first place and any functional use over and above that. It is also inherent in his office as the leader of the flock that he be active in motivating and guiding the church as it decides to begin a building program. However, his office does not warrant his assuming the responsibility of the church to build its own building. The pastor is not the church; the building will not be his when it is finished. The members of the corporation are the church and must assume all responsibility. Therefore, once the program has begun, the pastor must be careful to limit himself to serve only as a consultant. As such he should:

- introduce concepts and ideas;
- advise as to the coordination necessary between the corporation and its committees; and
- advise as to the safeguards necessary to insure the church that any program adopted would not incorporate non-biblical practices.

Although he is a consultant to the entire building program he must keep himself from becoming a source of final authority to the church or to the builder, and he must not permit himself to become an errand boy.

Only thus can the church assume its own responsibilities and reap all the benefits a building program should provide.

Role of professional builders and architects within the church.

If a corporation has within itself the craftsmanship to construct the entire building, it may well do so as a community project to God's glory. If, however, the corporation only has a few craftsmen as members, it is wise to disqualify them from working on the building as sub-contractors or even as the general contractor.

If a corporation does decide to permit members who are craftsmen to bid on the work, those members should resign from the building and finance committees before being permitted to bid. They must then remain off the committees throughout the entire building project then under construction, regardless of whether or not they are employed.

It is even wise not to place professionals from the church as members on the building or finance committee. However, their expertise should be used by making them consultants to the committees.

Role of the professional fund raiser.

The possibility of giving the task of raising funds to an outside professional must be weighed with great deliberation before it is adopted. The businesslike approach of such a professional is commendable. However, in many instances these men use a high-pressure method of quotas per family which could well defeat the very goal for which it is being used. Also, there is always the possibility that the spiritual concern necessary in dealing with babes in Christ will not be sufficiently honored.

However, this approach should not be automatically ruled out, especially if the program is to cost several hundred thousand dollars or more. Of course the control of the program can never be given *carte blanche* to a business concern. If this approach is adopted, therefore, the terms of the contract and the areas of responsibility of the professional must be determined and agreed upon before any contracts are signed.

Keeping the record on film.

One idea that has sufficient merit to propose to each church is to appoint an individual or a small committee to keep a pictorial record of each phase of the building program and of each development in the various phases. It is not only of great historical value in the years ahead, it also can be a source of information in the future for clarifying the relationship of the building(s) to the declaration of purpose.

THE CHURCH BUILDING PROGRAM, STEP-BY-STEP

The interplay of the corporation, building committee and finance committee and the general flow of the work from one to the other have been charted (See chart one). Each point on the chart is numbered. The discussion following the chart is designed to explain the value and use of each step, and is identified by its corresponding number.

It should be evident that the constitution and bylaws, the decision whether to have the finance committee be the trustees, the size of the corporation, and the size and cost of the proposed building will all be additional factors that may well cause the chart to be modified to fit a local situation. The general flow of the work will nonetheless be along the lines charted.

Discussion of the Chart

1. *Spiritual preparation to begin a building program.* From the beginning to the end the pastor and the elders must share several convictions in order to have a successful building program:

- the proposal of a building program is a necessity (or very shortly will be) and the church will suffer spiritually without it;
- the building program must be so developed that everything about it will be done only for the glory of God;
- and especially, no one individual may be permitted to dominate the program (whether by donations or through work volunteered).

These convictions demand several prerequisites:

- a spiritual bond of trust and confidence between pastor, officers and people. (If that bond is weak or missing, a building program must not be started with the hope of developing a spiritual bond: this does not work!);
- at least a general agreement among all the people that a building program is really a necessity;
- an in-depth review of the declaration of purpose, recommunicating its major facets to the members, in order to ensure that the building plan ultimately accepted will help to fulfill the specific purpose;
- leadership by the pastor (with the approval of and under the direction of the elders) to stimulate interest and enthusiasm for the program;
- a great and continuing prayer effort by the entire church. The time necessary to accomplish this spiritual preparation will vary in every place, but could never be much less than four months.

2. *Trustees.* Ultimately the trustees should draft a formal proposal to the corporation, requesting the corporation to authorize the establishment of a building program to structure the building committee and the finance committee, and to designate their specific responsibilities and limitations. (These instructions can be enlarged and/or amended later if it seems wise to do so.) Finally, the trustees must officially call a corporation meeting.

3. *Corporation meeting.* The corporation must act on the recommendations of the trustees. If affirmative action is taken, the program then is initiated.

4. *Finance committee.* This will be the first major study of the sources of finances available to the church. As was pointed out in an earlier chapter, two prerequisites for borrowing funds are that the income of the church has been maintained in a consistent fashion (e.g., there has been no big slump during the summer) in order to assure the loaner of a high degree of commitment on the part of the church members, and that the giving has basically been representative of all the members, not just of one or two individuals. Now, assuming these prerequisites, the committee must investigate the traditional loan, the church bonding approach and the simple promissory note.* Simultaneously, they must prepare for a drive to: (1) collect as many capital gifts as possible, and (2) collect as many pledges as possible.

A rule of thumb relative to pledges and mortgages that apparently works quite well will be inserted here as background material for the finance committee to consider:

a. Pledges should have a maximum duration of three years. (Most pledges are made for only one year, some for two years.)

b. If the pledges are sufficient to cover at least 85% of the mortgage for the first year, it is probable that the giving will be maintained for the first two to three years.

c. If the giving has in fact been sufficient to pay the mortgage for the first three years, the giving will probably be sufficient to pay for the entire mortgage.

—text continues on page 175

---

* These types of loans will be discussed at the conclusion of this chapter.

Chart I: A Church Building Program Step-By-Step

SPIRITUAL PREPARATION
to begin a building program

TRUSTEES
Propose the concept of entering into a building program

CORPORATION
1. Authorize concept of a Building Program
2. Set up:
    a. Finance Committee
    b. Building Committee
    c. Job descriptions and Limitations

FINANCE COMMITTEE
● Study sources of financing
● Prepare for capital gift drive
● Prepare for signed pledges

BUILDING COMMITTEE
Locate possible
sites for the church

TRUSTEES
1. Study both reports
2. Relay both reports to corporation
3. Make recommendations on both reports

SPIRITUAL PREPARATION
for decision

CORPORATION
1. Decide; if affirmative
2. Authorize trustees to act

SPIRITUAL ORIENTATION
of the program to collect the funds

TRUSTEES
1. Take necessary steps for care of property
2. Make rough estimate of money the corporation might make available for a building

BUILDING COMMITTEE
Determine how professional help (architect, general contractor, etc.) will be used

TRUSTEES
1. Study the report
2. Relay
3. Make recommendations

SPIRITUAL PREPARATION
for decision

CORPORATION
1. Decide; if affirmative,
2. Empower trustees to act

FINANCE COMMITTEE
- Study sources of financing
- Prepare for capital gift drive
- Prepare for signed pledges

BUILDING COMMITTEE
- Develop a master plan
- Develop initial drawings of first building
- Develop estimated cost

TRUSTEES
- Study and relay all proposals
- Recommend methods of financing
- Produce brochure of a building and financial recommendations

SPIRITUAL PREPARATION
for decision

CORPORATION
Note: probably conduct several meetings, with no power
of motion or vote, before making any decision.
1. Decide in general; if affirmative.
2. Authorize trustees to act.

FINANCE COMMITTEE
Draft specific plans for financing

BUILDING COMMITTEE
- Develop detailed drawings
- Secure firm bids

TRUSTEES
- Study specific financing proposals and firm bid costs
- Make specific recommendations to corporation

SPIRITUAL PREPARATION
for decision

CORPORATION
1. Make decision on specific proposals
2. Authorize trustees to act

SPIRITUAL ORIENTATION
of the program to collect the funds

SPIRITUAL CHALLENGE
Ground Breaking Exercises
and
Cornerstone Laying Exercises

BUILDING COMMITTEE
Actual Construction

TRUSTEES
Take necessary steps for the care of the
property and the use of the building

SPIRITUAL CHALLENGE
Dedication of Building

For additional buildings
repeat steps 10 through 29

d. Additional mortgages are possible after the first few years on the premise that the initial amount pledged has been given and new members could be challenged with a new building project. The finance committee should report its recommendations to the corporation by way of the trustees.

5. *Land committee or building committee.* The major task to be accomplished at this juncture is to locate land that will lend itself to the purpose decided on by the church. Many churches do not activate a building committee for this task; rather, they set up a land committee and, in many cases, simply ask the trustees themselves to locate the land in order to expedite the work.

This can sometimes be a long and discouraging task, especially if the finances are limited. Some guidelines might help:

- Locate the general area in which the church is interested.
- Within that area, locate several possibilities, and get definite boundary markings for them.
- If necessary, locate the owners of these properties from the files of the tax assessor's office.
- Consider a proposal to some of these owners which would permit them a tax deductible grant and benefit the church with a lower cost.
- Follow through with some of these proposals, preferably without a real estate agent as a middleman.
- Continue looking for additional leads, using real estate men to locate them.
- Be prepared, financially and by legal action of the corporation, to place option money on a piece of ground that seems favorable.

6. *Trustees.* Each of the reports—finance and land—should be carefully studied. Reactions of the trustees should be placed before the committees for their careful consideration. This may necessitate several re-draftings of the committee recommendations to the corporation. The trustees are then bound to relay the reports of the committees to the corporation. They may report their own recommendations as well. All the possible legal requirements upon which

these proposals will depend must be prepared for by professional legal counsel, so that any action taken by the corporation will be both proper and complete. The trustees must officially call a corporation meeting. The proposals should be circulated throughout the church well before the meeting is held.

7. *Spiritual preparation for decision.* The pastor and elders must be sure that several facets of the program are in focus before the corporation meeting, namely, that:
   - the prayer effort is being maintained;
   - the members have had ample opportunity personally to be abreast of the details;
   - the members have actually seen the land (several tours may have to be organized);
   - the members are challenged to begin to determine what part they can take by way of gifts and pledges.

8. *Corporation meeting.* The corporation must act on the proposals before it. If the decision is affirmative the necessary legal steps to authorize the action will be presented by the trustees for adoption.

9. *Spiritual orientation of the program to collect the funds.* The pastor and elders are again involved at this point, although the actual work is done by the trustees. Messages on stewardship are in order, along with the biblical imperative for commitment of all that we have and are to the work of the Lord. A church-oriented version of the faith promise plan, including foreign and home missions, church operating cost and building fund, is occasionally used to relate giving to the challenge of faith.

Several necessary features of this phase of the work are:
   - The pastor and church officers must visit each family of the church regarding the project, particularly the finances, and include a challenge to give as part of the work of God's kingdom.
   - In some instances, several rallies and special speakers could be used in connection with the beginning and then the end of the fund-raising drive. Also, the use of a "thermometer" to indicate the degree of achievement attained is worthwhile.
   - Some special activity or service at a pre-set date chosen for tallying the gifts and pledges must be provided in order to give

the fund raising its proper sense of spiritual movement and achievement.

Simultaneously, pledge cards* are distributed. They must be easily understood; they should include an opportunity to record a gift to be given as well as the pledge to be made. Since these pledges probably will have to be signed in order to be honored by a bank or building and loan institution, a place for the signature of the pledger should be provided.

10. *Trustees.* There are two jobs now before the trustees. The first must be done immediately. The second should be at least started, but the local situation will dictate the speed with which the work must be done.

a. Care of the property should be provided immediately.

- Erect a sign on the property.
- Arrange for proper care of the grounds, e.g., cut weeds in the summer, shovel snow in the winter, etc.
- Purchase adequate liability insurance to cover accidents and emergencies.
- Establish channels of communication with the neighbors, particularly those owning property contiguous to the church property, so that matters of common interest can be attended to.
- Study possible uses of the land for any benefits of the church even before a building is started.

b. Make a rough estimate of the amount of money the corporation might vote to make available for a building.

Motion towards a building may be slow immediately after land has been acquired, but it must not stop.

Before any more specific planning can be done a general idea is needed of the amount of money that will be available for the building. Tl.is must be regarded only as a rough estimate by the trustees, the corporation and the building committee; if it becomes too firm a figure, future developments will probably be

---

* See Appendix F for sample.

hampered. The consideration of several factors will assist the trustees in making a judgment:

- the cost of the building (excluding the value óf the land) that will ultimately be the major sanctuary is usually between two and one half to four times the average cost of a house *and* lot in the immediate neighborhood: e.g., in a neighborhood in which the average cost of a home and lot is $25,000, the church sanctuary may well cost between $62,500 and $100,000;
- the general demands that may result from the declaration of purpose;
- the average income of the members of the church;
- known factors such as wills, trusts, etc., which will become available to the church in a reasonable time;
- the anticipated growth rate of the church;
- a calculation (using square foot or cubic foot estimations) based on local building costs;
- a judgment of the reaction of the neighborhood to a multiple stage building program (in two or three stages) as compared to completing the entire building program in one operation;
- if a multiple stage building program is chosen, each unit that is built should be designed primarily to be used in the manner called for it in the master plan, and very little "bric-a-brac" should be used to doctor up a building to camouflage the fact that it must have a multiple use for a period of time; e.g., do not spend money on a small steeple for a building that is ultimately only to be an educational building; let the steeple wait until the sanctuary is built.

It would be wise to consult with the building committee and with the members of the corporation during the process of making this rough estimate. Also, it is very advisable to make known the figure and the logic used to arrive at the figure.

11. *Building committee.* The building program now is getting to the place where professional help is needed. There are various ways in which professional help is used by churches. The major ways are

outlined below. It must be understood that this is not intended to be an exhaustive study of this field, rather, it is intended to supply enough data so that the direction towards a more thorough investigation will be clear to the building committee. (At this point it is important to review the introductory material of this chapter, especially those paragraphs dealing with professionals within the church.)

* *The architect.* The following statement, taken directly from an architect's proposed contract to a church, defines his services. "The architect's professional services consist of the necessary conferences, the preparation of preliminary studies, working drawings, specifications, large scale and full size detail drawings, for architectural, structural, plumbing, heating, electrical, and other mechanical work; assistance in the drafting of forms of proposals and contracts; the issuance of certificates of payment; the keeping of accounts, the general administration of the business and supervision of the work."

It is customary that he will prepare the preliminary drawings without charge, as long as he is employed for the total job. His fee is usually a fixed percentage of the final cost of the church. If, however, he prepares the preliminary work, but is not employed for the total job, the architect usually charges an hourly rate for the work already done, and he may not release the drawings for the use of the church.

It is necessary to emphasize the esthetic value of the services of the architect as an artist and developer. It is necessary to have someone well qualified to combine the concepts in the declaration of purpose, the actual topography of the land, the financial potential of the church, and the materials of the building craft, to design the master plan and to design the actual building(s). The services of the architect in caring for such items as zoning restrictions, building permits, etc., are also of importance to the building committee.

Although it might seem to be a substantial savings to eliminate entirely the services of an architect by the "do-it-ourselves" approach, it is needed at least to prepare the master plan.

- *The general contractor.* His title easily defines his task: he is responsible for the actual building of the church. He is the responsible agent for the various sub-contractors. He must assure the quality of workmanship called for by the drawings and specifications.

  It is customary to pay him a percentage of the total cost. It is usually paid in thirds, at the completion of each third of the work.

- *Arrangements between the architect and general contractor.* Normally, the architect and the general contractor are not in the same corporation. The architect establishes channels of communication and is the responsible liaison between the building committee and the general contractor.

  Occasionally, the architect does have a business relationship with the general contractor; in such cases he is usually his employer or partner. The logic of this arrangement is that sooner or later every contract demands a degree of mutual trust; therefore, since it will be needed anyway, it should be exercised even in this area, thereby also permitting a savings by having architect and contractor staffs overlap, payroll accounting overlap, etc. The building committee must decide between these two arrangements.

  Another arrangement sometimes possible is to employ an architect not related to the church but to use a church member to serve as a general contractor, or vice-versa.

- *The "church building in a package" method.* There are several "package" building programs available on the market. This approach may save money. However, it must be thoroughly investigated and very carefully related to the concepts of the declaration of purpose, since it almost completely restricts local creativity. These "packages" are advertised in most Christian periodicals. The firms will usually send their representatives to call on the building committee.

- *Company of management specialists.* This kind of company is usually a small group of management specialists, each in one of

three major divisions: • design
                          • construction and supervision
                          • accounting

The unique feature of this approach is that the responsibility for the building program stays in the hands of the building committee rather than being in the hands of the architect.

This approach is relatively new and at present is advertised in only a few Christian periodicals.

General comment: When the building committee makes its study of various methods of proceeding and of the professionals who might be employed by the church, it should insist on seeing projects already completed by the professional under consideration and should correspond with his references. Preliminary discussion with officers of local banks and building and loan institutions about the individual under consideration is in order as well.

12. *Trustees.* The trustees must study the report of the building committee in detail and discuss it with the building committee. They should then relay the report to the corporation along with their own recommendations as to the report itself; as to the advisability of empowering the building committee to sign contracts with the professionals to be employed or to limit this authority to the trustees; and as to a maximum amount of funds available with which to accomplish the preliminary work.

13. *Spiritual preparation for decision.* The pastor and elders must be sure that:
   • the prayer effort is being maintained;
   • the members have had ample opportunity personally to be abreast of the details;
   • the spiritual condition of the church is healthy;
   • there is ample opportunity for any differences of opinion to be freely stated but such statements are free from personal innuendos.

   If the pastor and elders are not reasonably confident that the church is spiritually ready, they may recommend that no formal action be taken at the meeting or that the meeting be postponed.

14. *Corporation.* See paragraph number 8.

15. *Finance committee.* Develop along the same outline as given in paragraph number 4.
16. *Building committee.* The planning accomplished at this juncture is fundamental to the entire future development of the church. Therefore, it is *mandatory* that the building committee be prepared to have as many "think" sessions as necessary, regardless of the time consumed by them, in order to produce the program that most adequately meets all the prerequisites adopted by the church as to its purpose and its finances.

The work of the committee will include:

- consultations with the pastor and the architect relative to the concepts of the declaration of purpose;
- review of the relationship between the land and the declaration of purpose;
- provision of all technical data needed by the architect for his work (e.g., topographical surveys, land boring examinations, area growth potential, etc.);
- development of the master plan;
- development of the initial drawings for the first unit;
- development of an estimated cost (Note: if the square of the wall is above eight feet from the floor, it is very wise to use a cubic footage estimation rather than a square footage estimation);
- development of an estimated cost for landscaping;
- consideration of the interior furnishings (Experience shows that these furnishings will add approximately 10% to the cost of the building).

The initial drawings should at least include:

- a floor plan
- front and side elevations
- a water color perspective drawing.

The initial drawings may also be used to produce a scale model.

While discussing these initial drawings, several features must be considered which often are overlooked:

- The anticipated growth of the church for several years ahead should be factored in.
- Bottlenecks in the flow of traffic in corridors, etc., especially at rush moments on Sundays, should be smoothed out.
- If a multiple stage building program is planned, flexibility for the future use of or expansion of the first unit should be sought.

17. *Trustees.* The financial and building plans must be carefully studied, which usually demands several meetings with the respective committees in order fully to understand all the proposals and to formulate any recommendations the trustees may want to make. More time will then be needed to discuss these proposals with the committees, to receive back their reactions and finally to refine the initial recommendations for presentation to the corporation.

It must be pointed out that the trustees normally make firm recommendations to the corporation only about the report of the finance committee, with only general comments regarding the building committee's report. However, if the trustees conclude that the intentions of the corporation have been neglected or distorted in the final proposals of the building committee, this conclusion must be transmitted to the corporation.

If there are no major unsolvable differences between the two committees and the trustees, it is of great value for the trustees to produce a brochure explaining the building program and the financial plans to fund it. This is an absolutely necessary tool if the building is at all expensive.

The trustees must officially call for a corporation meeting. It is often very useful to call for several meetings at which only discussion is possible before having the meeting at which voting will take place.

18. *Spiritual preparation for decision.* Same as paragraph number 13, in addition to which all recommendations for the building program must be carefully and publicly assessed so that the corporation will be prepared to step out on faith but not to presume on God. In this respect the pastor must motivate his officers to use spiritual discernment in determining their recommendations for the members. This is particularly pertinent as to the degree of aggressive

leadership they will choose to exert (individually and/or collectively) either for or against the proposals.

19. *Corporation.* Several non-voting meetings may be conducted. At the meeting in which the voting is to take place, special care should be exercised that the meeting is properly called and a quorum is present. The actions called for are:

    a. approval of the master plan for development;

    b. approval of the preliminary design of the first building;

    c. approval of the estimated cost figures proposed;

    d. approval of the plans for securing the funds for construction;

    e. when these approvals are made, authorization of the building committee to have the detailed drawings and specifications of the first building prepared and to secure firm bids for the construction;

    f. authorization of the finance committee to draft specific plans and prepare necessary contracts, etc., for final approval for the financing of the construction.

    It may be that the corporation will do only part of this at first (for instance: authorize the detailed drawings and specifications for the first building). The corporation must act in such a way that it is really stepping out on faith and that the ultimate decision is really that of the people themselves.

20. *Finance committee.* Draft in detail the plans for raising the necessary funds and prepare the necessary contracts, etc., for final approval by the corporation to put the plans into operation.

21. *Building committee.* Proceed to have the detailed drawings and specifications for the first building prepared. Following the procedure previously adopted by the corporation (see paragraph number 8), secure firm bids for the cost of construction.

22. *Trustees.* Study the reports of the finance and building committees, formulate recommendations to the committees and meet to determine if refinements in the proposals are necessary. Transmit the proposals of the committees, along with their own recommendations, to the corporation. They must ascertain exactly what legal steps are necessary in that state (particularly as to the wording of motions authorizing banks to make loans, etc.) and be prepared

to present these to the corporation. They must officially call a corporation meeting.

23. *Spiritual preparation for decision.* See paragraph number 18.
24. *Corporation.* The corporation must take the following actions:
    a. approval of the detailed drawings and specifications for the first building;
    b. approval of the detailed plans for raising the necessary funds and for the terms of the proposed contracts;
    c. if these approvals are given, authorization of the trustees to proceed with the program.
25. *Spiritual orientation of the program to collect the funds.* See paragraph number 9.
26. *Spiritual challenge: ground-breaking exercises and cornerstone-laying exercises.* Every church should seek opportunities publicly to show the relationship between its faith, hope and praise and the building program. Ground-breaking exercises and cornerstone-laying exercises provide just such opportunities. Through the newspaper coverage an additional advantage can be gained: extended public exposure of the church.
27. *Building committee.* The actual construction will demand much of the members of the building committee, especially in conjunction with the supervision of the quality of the workmanship.

One pitfall that must be pointed out is the desire to make changes in the plans during the time of construction. Changes of a minor sort (e.g., changes in the color scheme) can be made without too much difficulty. Major changes (e.g., adding an additional room; changing from an "A" roof to a hip roof) may be very expensive indeed. Any proposed change must be agreed upon by the building committee, not decided by the one delegated as liaison officer. Also, if a proposed change will seriously change the looks, functions and/or the cost of the building, the entire corporation must give its approval before the change can be authorized.

If volunteer labor is to be used, it is the responsibility of the building committee to see that it is done on time so that related work is not delayed. Also, it is responsible to be sure the quality of workmanship is satisfactory.

If parts of the building or equipment in the building will need special maintenance after the church takes over the building, the building committee is responsible that these instructions are transmitted from the contractor to the personnel of the church to be charged with that task.

The building committee must be satisfied with the functioning of all the equipment connected with the building as well as the quality of workmanship on the building itself before it releases the contractor.

28. *Trustees.* The trustees must prepare for the church to assume the responsibility for the building at its completion. This includes adequate insurance, care of the grounds, maintenance of the building and rules for the use of the building.

29. *Spiritual challenge: dedication of the building.* The program of the service of dedication is almost completely self-explanatory. Other aspects of the occasion, however, are often overlooked. Some of them are:

- The public press should be used as much as possible.
- All the professional men used should be properly recognized.
- Community officials should be used as much as possible.
- Throughout the service of dedication, clear and definite emphasis must be laid on the declaration of purpose.

LOANS: BANKS, BUILDING AND LOAN ASSOCIATIONS AND BOND ISSUES

It is not the design of this book to present an in-depth study of the principles and economics of these sources of borrowed money. Rather, it is the purpose to introduce each in a general way so that any church will have sufficient knowledge at least to proceed to its own in-depth study.

CHART II: BORROWING MONEY IN ORDER TO BUILD

	BANKS; BUILDING AND LOAN ASSOCIATIONS	BOND ISSUES
COLLATERAL NEEDED	Cash available is usually limited to 65% (maximum) of collateral offered to secure the loan.	Subject to state restrictions, the amount of collateral offered is usually set arbitrarily by the seller. It is often that minimum amount which the seller assumes the proposed purchasing market will demand.
ABILITY TO OBTAIN FUNDS	This depends on the policies and resources of each institution, and upon the current money market and economic situation, both locally and nationally.	Money will be obtainable from any number of sources, but mostly from members themselves. The amount sought is related to the church families' ability to loan, based on the number of families, per capita giving, income multipliers, church income, the economy of the local area, etc. Three major proposals may be offered under the title "bond": a. A promissory note: a local agreement, unregistered. b. A registered bond issue: much like the promissory note, but complying with all state regulations and registered with the state. c. A guaranteed bond issue: a registered bond issue, the sinking fund of which is underwritten by a separate organization (usually a national church agency of a denomination).
METHOD AND CAPACITY TO REPAY THE LOAN	Signed pledges are usually demanded to demonstrate ability to repay. Almost always, a straight-line program of amortization is fol-	Signed pledges are usually demanded to demonstrate ability to pay, plus an in-depth objective financial survey. Often an "inverted S-curve" amortization is followed. For example:

lowed. For example:

A $50,000 note at X% interest is repayable at $Y.00 per week, each week, until the principal is repaid.

A $50,000 bond issue at X% interest is repayable at:
$1/2 Y.00 per week for the first year; $2/3 Y.00 per week for the second year; $3/4 Y.00 per week for the third year; $Y.00 per week for the fourth year; $1 1/3 Y.00 per week for the fifth year and thereafter.

This permits the church to build when its income is low, and to use the church building itself to enhance the outreach into the area.

COST

1. An interest rate set by the institution.

2. An initial service charge (sometimes referred to as "points") which depends on the policy of the institution.

3. Particular expense accounts, such as:
● appraisal fee
● credit report fee
● title policy
● survey fee
● recording fee
The initial service charge and particular expense accounts usually total 3%-4% of the loan.

1. The lowest possible interest rate that will sell the issue to the proposed purchasing market.

2. Service fees, to include some of the particular expense accounts as are used by the banks; plus registration fees, cost of printing the bonds, bank arrangements for handling the sinking fund, amortization and bond-denomination tables, training in selling the bonds, etc. This usually comes to about 6% of the bond issue.

3. For guaranteed bond issues, a breakdown different from that listed in No. 2 above, but usually amounting to the same total cost, about 6% of the bond issue.

19

The Particular Church:
Mother-Daughter and Church Satellite Programs

These programs have been singled out for discussion here since they are unusual means of development and do not logically fall into the discussion in chapter seven. However, it is not the author's purpose to describe the programs in exhaustive detail. This presentation will simply survey the programs and highlight the key factors.

DEFINITIONS

The mother-daughter church program is a method of establishing a new particular church by using members of an existing church as the nucleus for the work, with the encouragement and under the guidance of the existing church, and often with its financial assistance. It has been used many times.

On the other hand, the church satellite program is a new concept. Its aim is development of any number of worship and outreach groups in the neighborhoods surrounding an existing church, whose participants:

- become or continue as members of the existing church;
- continue under the discipline of the existing church;
- worship on a regularly scheduled basis in the existing church (e.g., at least every other Sunday evening);
- support the special activities of the existing church;
  but;

- conduct all of their stated meetings (with the exception of those scheduled to be with the existing church) in private homes or rented facilities in their own neighborhood;
- also conduct Sunday School, children's work, Bible classes, and special outreach programs in their own neighborhood.

The term "church satellite" is the author's. It is his conviction that this approach to church extension should be widely used in the decade of the seventies. It is already being used in several places.

CONDITIONS CONDUCIVE TO CHURCH EXTENSION VIA THESE PROGRAMS

Condition: The existing church started with the policy to establish a mother-daughter program.

Some churches adopt a policy from the very beginning to multiply (note: not "split") into two churches when certain conditions are achieved. Experience has taught that it is often impossible really to "multiply" and not to "split" unless the principle has been integrated into the entire life of a church. On the other hand, when the members have been emotionally and organizationally prepared to accept this policy as simply the next major step in church growth, the transition from one church into a mother-daughter set of churches can be achieved quite easily.

Condition: The existing church has a very distinctive testimony.

It is often the case that a particular church has a distinctive emphasis which other churches in the area do not share. For instance, one church may emphasize a particular doctrine, while other churches in the neighborhood do not. More often, however, an evangelical church will emphasize biblical doctrines which are no longer maintained by the many churches which have substituted a program of social action alone for biblical truth. Because there is often only one such church in a very large geographical area, the membership usually comes from many neighborhoods in order to worship at that church. If the number of such people coming from a given neighborhood grows sufficiently, and especially if the neighborhood is a great distance from the existing church, the potential for a mother-daughter arrangement is great indeed.

Condition: The existing church is in a megalopolis or at least a major metropolitan area.

Megalopoloi are developing throughout the United States. They are defined by Webster's Dictionary as "very large cities." In the common use of the word, a megalopolis is an adjoining set of cities, often growing up along major traffic arteries, which either fan out from one very heavy population center or connect several very heavy population centers. In these situations, a wide-awake church can and should plan to establish a daughter church in each new community which arises as the megalopolis grows.

Condition: The existing church is in a town or in a city which will not connect with other cities to become part of a megalopolis.

The built-in limitations of these communities, especially if other churches are already present, make the church satellite program the ideal way to extend the church.

Condition: The existing church is in the inner city.*

The term "inner city" has become a technical term in today's vocabulary. An inner city is composed of many blighted neighborhoods, in each of which the residents find themselves "locked in" (i.e., unable to move away into better circumstances and often even unable to walk from one neighborhood to another) because of race, economics, prejudice and fear of reprisal. In such situations it is virtually impossible for one church, regardless of its distinctive character, to draw people from more than one neighborhood. Rather, until the "locking in" bars are broken, a church in each neighborhood will be needed. One existing church could use the satellite program as an ideal way to meet this need. One of the goals of this program must of course be to preach and live the gospel in order to break down the "locking in" bars. Only as the evangelical church undertakes such a program will it begin to assume any of its responsibility to be a potent force in effecting this breakthrough. (The author must point out that these comments are the result of a careful, extensive and on-the-field study of the inner city for well over a year, with personal observation of much good that is now being done, but that he has not, at this writing, had the privilege of personally directing such an inner city program.)

---

* The subject of the inner city church will not be developed in this book.

THE MOTHER-DAUGHTER CHURCH PROGRAM

This program is a potential tool for every church. When attendance gets too large, most churches first consider conducting two morning services. But churches should consider the mother-daughter arrangement first, especially since the over all theory of this program is quite easy to communicate to all the members.

It has already been stressed, however, that the application of this program has the latent ability to "split" a church. If at the very beginning the established church adopted a program to direct its anticipated growth along these lines, the potential of this being an experience of multiplication rather than of division (a split) is much greater. This requires regular pastoral teaching, both from the pulpit and in private, of the biblical basis for the existence and extension of the church and for the responsibility of every Christian to be involved in the ministry of the church.

When it seems possible that a daughter church might be established, preliminary preparations must be made:

- locate one area as a probable immediate goal, and other areas as possible future goals;
- conduct frequent congregational meetings to evaluate the progress toward accomplishing the immediate goal and to assess the implications to the members and work of the existing church;
- establish a fund, supported by the entire church, to assist the daughter church in a major way at its beginning;
- and most important of all, lead the congregation regularly in prayer for God's blessing upon the church, in such a way that each family in the initial church is itself involved in prayer before God to determine its own responsibility, whether to remain in the mother church or to step out with the daughter church.

SPECIFIC PREPARATIONS FOR THE BEGINNING OF THE DAUGHTER CHURCH

Several prerequisites must be fulfilled before the decision to establish a daughter church can be made:

- at least eight seed families in the existing church already live in the area in which the daughter church is to be established;

- the finances of the existing church are not in a precarious condition at the time the decision to establish the daughter church is made (Note: the prior commitment to this method of church development will have influenced the size of debts and obligations the existing church will have assumed);
- a survey of the proposed area has been made and its findings indicate that a daughter church would be able to grow;
- Bible classes and some kind of children's work have already been started in the area.

But the fact that these prerequisites have been met may not automatically be considered sufficient grounds on which to proceed. The congregation of the existing church must share a sense of conviction that God is indeed placing this step on their hearts. There should be a spirit of anticipation and excitement within the entire congregation as this step of faith is undertaken. No amount of planning and organizing will ever take the place of the power of God and the appreciation of his blessing.

When, however, the prerequisites have been fulfilled and the spiritual preparations are evidently complete, the congregation of the existing church must vote, at a properly called meeting, that the plans to establish a daughter church be drawn up in detail and that the pastor, elders and trustees be authorized to process them.

Next, it is wise, after calling the organizing pastor of the daughter church, to have him serve for several months as the associate pastor of the mother church before he assumes the responsibility of leading the seed families out as the daughter church. During this time he may serve in various ways in the existing church in order to become acquainted with it and its programs, to have time to develop the necessary rapport with the seed families themselves, to become oriented to the proposed area in which the daughter church will be established, to teach the Bible classes in that area, to begin to cultivate his own contacts in the area, to look for a place in which to begin services, and to look for proposed sites for the purchase of property for the church.

Plans should be made to use the people of the existing church to conduct some combination of the programs described in chapter six in order to locate additional seed families and start a list of prime contacts for the daughter church to develop.

Also, plans should be made to determine the best means of oversight of the daughter church. Very probably the elders of the mother church will appoint two of their members to act as the borrowed elders. If there are still at least six additional elders in the mother church, the committee on assessment may also be appointed from their ranks. Most often the inclination at this time is for the daughter church simply to continue under the mother church eldership as if it were still part of the one congregation. Although there is no reason to say this is improper, experience has demonstrated that it is not as practical as it appears.

- The daughter church is facing new and specialized problems which, to a great degree, do not exist for the mother church; these problems cannot be satisfied by merely using the programs at work in the mother church. Consequently, adequately to analyze and solve these problems will demand a great deal of time from the eldership of the mother church, and experience shows that they seldom find the necessary time.
- On the other hand, the mother church is facing its own problem: the loss of these seed families. This necessitates some major adjustments, which again consume a great deal of the elders' time.
- Finally, the daughter church, being much smaller, is aware of each problem as soon as it arises and therefore believes it needs constant, almost immediate care, so that it easily interprets any delay in such care as a case of "out of sight, out of mind." This attitude usually develops tension between the two churches, even though the program started with the best possible relationships.

Special channels of communication for handling finances, overlapping of programs, etc., must be set up and put into immediate practice. One that should be mentioned is the necessity to provide the seed families of the daughter church with a means of returning to the mother church if that is felt to be best for the family. On the one hand, the procedure must be difficult enough that a seed family is forced to make a careful decision, not just an emotional one. Thus the daughter church can really depend on all its families. On the other hand, the procedure must be easy enough to permit the seed family which has made a valid decision to return to the mother church to do so without embarrassment. It would be wise for the family to be counseled by the elders of the mother church prior to its return. The most evident valid reason for a return to the mother church is in order to meet a particular need of the children of the family which the daughter church proves unable yet to satisfy.

Finally, when the daughter church is established as a mission church and then later as a particular church, special services appropriate to the occasion should be conducted.

THE CHURCH SATELLITE PROGRAM

This program will provide an opportunity for men (who are members of the particular church but not necessarily elders) and even for entire families to develop leadership and to be used as they never could be simply as members of a large congregation at worship. Thus those accepting responsibility for the satellite ministries will themselves be blessed and almost always will mature spiritually, usually at an exceptionally fast pace. It will also foster the development of many creative talents (musical, artistic, etc.) which would not be used when submerged in the larger congregation.

This program will satisfy the desire of our particular age for worship that is personal, often in small groups, providing a great degree of individual participation plus an informal relationship among the families involved.* Yet it does this without severing ties with an established church which can offer many kinds of needed help during emergencies and also maintain both administrative and judicial discipline.

This program will permit the small satellite group to maintain an active children's and young people's program (as distinguished from the Sunday School program) through the established church even though they themselves often would not have enough young people to have their own independent program.

---

* The degree of informality must not be permitted to distort the worship of the group.

Prerequisites.

Very little of the detailed preparation necessary to establish a daughter church is needed in this program. The spiritual preparation of the established church will, of course, be necessary, and the same sense of conviction is needed for this program as for that one.

So long as this sense of conviction has evidently been placed on the hearts of all the members of the established church, the preparations for starting satellites are primarily matters of communication. Two areas must be agreed on by all before any satellite is started. They are the purpose for the satellite and the limitation of the authority of the satellite and of those in it.

The purpose is implicit in the definition given at the beginning of this chapter. It could be stated as follows:

> The satellite exists as a part of and as the continuing responsibility of a particular church. Its overall purpose is to provide a ministry for members of the particular church in a given neighborhood. This ministry will be very personal in all of its aspects because of the limited size of the group and the consequent interdependence of all the members. The specific purposes of the work are: to conduct worship services (tailored to the small size of the group, but without loss of any of the basic parts and attitudes of true worship), to conduct programs of outreach to the families in the neighborhood, and to afford meaningful relationships among the families of the group.

The limitation of the authority of the satellite includes the following aspects:

- The satellite is not to be developed as a small particular church; if a local satellite seems to be developing such a potential, it must be dealt with as a daughter church, with all the necessary preparations, expenses, etc.

- The men serving in the satellite may not assume the privileges and prerogatives of an ordained minister.

- All matters of discipline (administrative and/or judicial) must be dealt with by the elders of the established church.

- The sacraments may be administered in the satellite group only with proper provision by the established church.

PARTICULAR CHURCH—SATELLITE ARRANGEMENTS

The particular church which sets out to establish satellite groups must be prepared to have its pastor spend a block of his time with the men who are speaking at the satellites. It is the responsibility of the elders of the particular church to be sure, on the one hand, that no heresy is inadvertently taught, and on the other hand, that solid spiritual food is given to those attending the satellite group. The elders are therefore ultimately responsible to maintain a constant teaching ministry to the speakers, but they will usually expect the pastor to carry it out. Much of it can be done by loaning the speakers key books to study and by conducting teaching sessions. However it is done, instruction must be regularly given.

Coupled with this demand on the pastor's time is the fact that the satellites will be reaching more and more new people. After sufficient contact has been made with them, the pastor will need to visit them to discuss the responsibilities of confessing one's faith, of membership, etc. These tasks are exactly in conformity with the Scriptures ("And the things that thou hast heard of me among many witnesses, the same commit thou to faithful men, who shall be able to teach others also" II Timothy 2:2), so that the particular church should rejoice in this work. Also, it should be pointed out that the financial support given by the satellite groups themselves may well make it possible for the particular church to employ an assistant or an associate pastor.

One of the basic tenets of this program of development is that the people of the satellite will worship on a regularly scheduled basis in the particular church under the ministry of the pastor. This might mean that the particular church will have to have two morning services, with some of the satellite groups coming to the early service, others coming to the later service, and still others coming to the evening service.

The financial responsibilities of this ministry will have to be worked out carefully. It is suggested that the satellite groups do receive offerings, all of which must be accounted for through the particular church's treasury for purposes of tax shelter. A procedure must be developed which will permit the satellite to use its own funds for developing its own programs and for at least some of its own mission interests, all of which, however, must at least be approved by the particular church. The procedure must also include some participation by the satellite in supporting the programs and obligations of the particular church, including the basic building program and support of the pastor.

As to the officers of the particular church, some should be active in the satellite groups.

The satellite group should organize an administrative committee (see chapter ten, especially the comments regarding steering committees).

In most cases, the young people of the satellite groups will belong to the young people's group of the particular church, so that this extremely necessary aspect of church life can be adequately cared for.

Often it is easier to establish a satellite group if a team of families of the particular church shoulders the responsibilities simultaneously. The need to prepare a sermon each week will demand a great deal of the time of the untrained laymen. Two men could do the work alternately. The same holds true for some of the tasks falling to the women of the group, such as preparing the house for the meeting each week.

Before a satellite group can be established, the pastor and the elders must first assure themselves that the man and family or the team of families taking the responsibilities are not only grounded in the basics of the faith and the government of the church, but are emotionally and physically capable of the additional load they will be called on to carry.

As for the Sunday School of the satellite groups, each situation will demand an individual arrangement. Sunday School should be a special delight for the participants, since it will allow very personal teaching conditions.

The pastor may teach the Bible classes during the week. However, as much as possible, the laymen of the satellite should be encouraged to teach them.

As to a mid-week children's work, each situation will demand an individual arrangement. This is an extremely important function of the program, however, and should not be overlooked simply because of the press of other matters.

The particular church must engage in a special prayer program for each of the satellite groups. It must provide special programs, meetings, training seminars, etc., for them and be responsive to any particular programs that may be requested by the satellites. It should encourage its people occasionally to attend some of the satellite services and be ready to offer their help when special needs arise.

Specialized groups such as men's councils or women's circles will continue on the particular church level and will provide a direct interplay between particular church and satellite.

In conclusion, it seems wise to point out again that this approach to church development should become a major factor in the culture of the future. Serious consideration must be given by every church to the satellite program before more and more dollars are spent for larger and larger buildings and the members become conversely less individual and significant.

Appendices

Appendices

A. SAMPLES OF THE ORDER OF WORSHIP FOR MORNING WORSHIP SERVICES.

A general format:
　　Prelude
　　Doxology
　　Invocation and Lord's Prayer
　　Hymn
　　Responsive Reading
　　Apostles' Creed
　　Gloria Patri
　　Scripture Reading
　　Pastoral Prayer
　　Announcements
　　Offering
　　Offertory-Special Music
　　Hymn
　　Sermon
　　Hymn
　　Benediction
　　Postlude
Some churches choose to title the hymns, often listing them as follows:
　　first hymn: "Hymn of Worship"
　　hymn before the message: "Hymn of Rejoicing"
　　hymn after the message: "Hymn of Testimony"

A non-structured topical format:
　　Welcome and Announcements
　　Prayer and Meditation
　　Call to Worship
　　Entrance Hymn
　　Prayer of Invocation
　　Apostles' Creed
　　Reading from God's Law
　　Prayer of Confession and Forgiveness
　　Scripture: Assurance of Pardoning Grace
　　Scripture Lesson
　　Sermon
　　Sermon Hymn
　　Pastoral Prayer*
　　Offering and Doxology
　　Hymn of Praise and Thanksgiving
　　Benediction
　　Silent Prayer

---

*This is often called "Congregational Prayer."

A structured topical format:
> Approach to God:
>> Prelude
>> Call to Worship
>> Hymn of Praise
>> Scripture: Confession of Need
>> Hymn of Forgiveness
>> Apostles' Creed
> Word of God:
>> Prayer
>> Scripture Lesson
>> Sermon
> Response to God:
>> (Lord's Supper)
>> Hymn of Worship
>> Offering
>> Prayer of Petition
>> Doxology
>> Benediction
>> Silent Prayer

B. THE ORGANIZING PASTOR.

Sources for locating the organizing pastor (depending on the nature and government of the proposed church):

- ministers of established churches;
- ministers laboring as chaplains, missionaries, church executives, evangelists, etc.;
- missionaries under church extension boards in denominations;
- recent graduates of Bible schools, Bible colleges and theological seminaries.

Locating an organizing pastor:

- In some denominations the procedure for locating an organizing pastor has already been specified.
- In all other cases the following procedure is suggested:
  First:
  - The committee on assessment locates a qualified candidate. (Note: the mission church can always make suggestions to the committee on assessment.)
  - The work is fully described to him.
  - If he is convinced, on the basis of all he knows, that he should become the organizing pastor he agrees:
    - to be proposed as the organizing pastor to the mission church;
    - to visit for several days to seek confirmation of his conviction.
  - But if, during the visit, some unforeseen problem becomes apparent, he has the right to veto the proposal immediately after the visit.

Next:

- The committee on assessment makes the proposal to the mission church, giving biographical and professional data, and arranges for any clarifications deemed necessary.
- If the mission church is convinced, on the basis of all it knows, that it should accept the proposed organizing pastor, the committee on assessment arranges for him to visit.
- But if, during the visit, some unforeseen problem becomes apparent, it has the right to veto the proposal immediately after the visit.

Finally:

- The organizing pastor labors in the mission church until it becomes a particular church.
- In one of the first congregational meetings of the particular church a proper call for a pastor is extended (probably to the organizing pastor), according to the procedures of the newly-adopted bylaws.
- The minister to whom the call has been extended and who has accepted it is installed as the first pastor of the church.

C. THE INTRODUCTORY BROCHURE.

This is a short brochure which describes the major facets of the mission church, with special emphasis on the specific purpose of the church. It should include statements on the Bible, the doctrine and government of the proposed church, and its role in the contemporary world. It must be colorful, attractive and easily read in a few minutes.

D. THE DETAILED BROCHURE.

This brochure will cover much of the same material as the introductory brochure, but in greater depth. It should be attractive and easily comprehended. It should at least include a comprehensive description of the particular purpose of the proposed church; references to any subordinate standards the proposed church will adopt; statements about doctrine, explained and supported by biblical references; statements about government, with specific references to illustrate any distinctive features; statements about the position of the proposed church with respect to other churches, the various councils of churches, etc.; a historical summary of the background of the proposed church (particularly if it is denominationally oriented); and possibly some features of related churches, schools and/or missionary activities.

E. AN EVALUATION SHEET FOR USE IN THE IN-DEPTH ORIENTATION SURVEY

Name...

Address...

Telephone.....................*Occupation*...............................

Approximate Age: Husband.........*Wife*..........

Names and approximate ages of children:

Give your estimation of the profession of faith made.

What is their church background? Are they presently members of any church?

Did they evidence any concern for the lost? Explain.

> *Estimate their degree of understanding of the following terms: (Insert a few significant terms which touch on the system of doctrine and form of government of the proposed mission church).*

> *Was there a sense of conviction evident concerning the proposal for a mission church in the area?*

> *List referral names and addresses:*

Other comments:

> *Name of interviewer*.......................

> *Date of interview*........................

F. THE PLEDGE CARD

MY FINANCIAL SUPPORT
for the
BUILDING PROGRAM

_____CHURCH

Gift .... $_____

Pledge .... $_____

My pledge is for_____ years.

_____   _____

Signature   **Date**

G. SAMPLE OF BYLAW FOR REMOVING A PASTOR

Section 1, Precautions:

a. The court of original jurisdiction for the pastor is the presbytery.
b. Before accusations are received by the Session, the following biblical injunctions must be emphasized: "Let the elders that rule well be counted worthy of double honour, especially they who labour in the word and doctrine" (I Timothy 5:17). "Against an elder receive not an accusation, but before two or three witnesses" (I Timothy 5:19). "Judge not, that ye be not judged. For with what judgment ye judge, ye shall be judged: and with what measure ye mete, it shall be measured to you again" (Matthew 7:1-2).
c. Before accusations are received by the Session, it must be evident that the biblical injunction of Matthew 18:15-17 has been observed in every situation in which it is applicable.
d. It must be remembered that the pulpit is never officially "vacant" until declared so by presbytery.

Section 2, Causes and Procedures:

a. Admitted immorality: The Session immediately may refuse the pulpit to the minister and must notify presbytery of the circumstance; then after due congregational action, the Session must appeal to presbytery to declare the pulpit vacant and to appoint a moderator.
b. Admitted heresy (only of cardinal points of the Reformed system of doctrine): Same as "a" above.

c. Accusations: The Session should seek to counsel with the pastor and, if it deems wise, request presbytery to assume the responsibility of trial and consequent action. (These actions must be done according to the procedures of the Book of Discipline.) The pastor normally would continue his ministry (since he has not been proven guilty) unless the Session and the pastor concur that the Lord's work will be hurt until the situation is resolved.

d. Cases having nothing to do with immortality or heresy: The Session (probably a Pastoral Relations Committee of the Session), and possibly other members of presbytery, must counsel directly and at extended length with the pastor and those of the congregation involved in order to achieve a remedy which, in effect, is a new and God-honoring degree of ministry; if that fails, after notifying the Clerk of Presbytery, and in strict accordance with the regulations of the church's constitution and bylaws, a congregational meeting may be called to consider voting on the dismissal of the pastor; a two-thirds vote of the membership, on the first and only ballot, will be necessary to finalize the action, and the voting, if the congregation does vote to dismiss the pastor, must be by secret ballot; then presbytery must be requested to declare the pulpit vacant and to appoint a moderator.

Index